pass the smiles
a better world, a happier you.

GREG KEAST
KEVIN KAOHELAULII

Copyright © 2010 by Greg Keast and Kevin Kaohelaulii

ISBN-13: 978-0-9845307-0-0
ISBN-10: 0-9845307-0-3

All rights reserved. No part of this book may be reproduced for any commercial purpose without the written consent of the authors. Portions may be reproduced for educational and non-profit purposes with a citation or reference.

Kahala Press
P.O. Box 88563
Honolulu HI 96830

*This book is dedicated to all those who make the effort
every day to pass the smiles and do something positive for others.*

Table of Contents

SECTION 1 - INTRODUCTION 9
Chapter 1: The enemy is formidable 11

SECTION 2 - ACTION 15
Chapter 2: The importance of action 17
Chapter 3: Change your behavior and thoughts will follow 19
Chapter 4: Write your top three goals in life 25
Chapter 5: Slow down 29
Chapter 6: Do something you enjoy and include someone 31
Chapter 7: Take time to relax each day 33
Chapter 8: Walking 35

SECTION 3 - BASELINES 37
Chapter 9: Adaptability 39
Chapter 10: Baselines 41
Chapter 11: Up the ante 45

SECTION 4 - BOMBARDMENT 49
Chapter 12: Under bombardment 51
Chapter 13: Stop or limit all news media 53

SECTION 5 - NEGATIVE 55
Chapter 14: What is negative? 57
Chapter 15: Drawn to the negative 59
Chapter 16: Creating a list of negative forces 61
Chapter 17: Manage and control all the negative 63
Chapter 18: Identify three areas for personal improvement ... 67
Chapter 19: Use negative emotions as signs 69

SECTION 6 - POSITIVE **71**

Chapter 20: What is positive?..73
Chapter 21: Create a list of positive forces....................................75
Chapter 22: Visualize your perfect self...77
Chapter 23: Experience one inspirational thing a day..................79
Chapter 24: Do nice little things for others....................................81
Chapter 25: Journaling the positive..83
Chapter 26: Fostering a positive environment...............................85
Chapter 27: Positive dream programming.....................................87

SECTION 7 - PEOPLE **89**

Chapter 28: It's all about relationships..91
Chapter 29: Be mindful of how you view others............................95
Chapter 30: People are like the weather..99
Chapter 31: The all-powerful smile...101
Chapter 32: Creating a personal legacy.......................................105
Chapter 33: See people as people and not as objects...............107
Chapter 34: Associate with many positive people......................111
Chapter 35: Stop associating with negative people...................113
Chapter 36: Make one person smile each day............................117
Chapter 37: Listen more..119
Chapter 38: Stop snapping...123

SECTION 8 - LANGUAGE **127**

Chapter 39: Be aware of the power of language.........................129
Chapter 40: Feel the feeling..133
Chapter 41: Do not use words that claim ownership..................135
Chapter 42: Limit the use of absolute words...............................139
Chapter 43: Do not use negative language.................................141

SECTION 9 - THOUGHTS **145**

Chapter 44: Thoughts are important but hard to change........................... 147
Chapter 45: Start each day with a positive thought................................... 151
Chapter 46: See these concepts in things you see everyday........................ 153
Chapter 47: Stop thinking negatively.. 155
Chapter 48: Redefine your past... 157
Chapter 49: Align yourself with yourself... 159
Chapter 50: Stay humble.. 163
Chapter 51: See good things in bad... 165
Chapter 52: Remember these key thoughts... 167
Chapter 53: Your energy is eternal 169
Chapter 54: End each day with a positive broadcast................................... 173

SECTION 10 - APPENDICES **175**

Appendix 1: Positive behaviors.. 177
Appendix 2: Enjoyable things to do... 179
Appendix 3: Nice little things you can do... 181
Appendix 4: Ideas for a personal legacy.. 183
Appendix 5: Daily reminders... 185

INTRODUCTION

CHAPTER 1
THE ENEMY IS FORMIDABLE

"Adversity introduces a man to himself."
Author Unknown

We hate to be the ones to say this, but things are much worse than you think.

"But hold on," you say, "I thought this was a book about happiness?"

It is, but first we've got some news for you.

In your quest for happiness, you are facing a formidable opponent, someone who knows you inside and out, someone who knows your every weakness, someone who knows your every move and will never give up. Who is it?

It's you.

That's right.

You are your own worst enemy in your quest for happiness.

How can that be?

Let us explain.

We like to think of ourselves as a collective whole, so when we say the word "I" we believe that we are referring to a single, solid, and solitary entity but that's simply not true.

We, that is, you and I, are composed of parts, physical and mental, yet not all of them are working together—in fact, some are in direct conflict.

The truth is from a psychological perspective what you call "you," what we call "you," is really a collection of competing interests and traits. Inside our personalities are positive and negative elements vying for control. The positive parts lift you up and see the world in a favorable light. The negative parts do not and rebel.

And so there is, contained within you, a perpetual conflict between negative and positive. What "you" represent is a battleground where the negative forces are trying to bring down the positive. You might not even know you *are* a war zone.

This conflict is universal and never-ending. It is not unique to you. Everyone has the same struggle and always will. Good and bad reside in all of us. The problem is the negative half has the upper hand and worse, has backup!

Here's why:

Your negative self has a tag-team partner and sympathetic ally in the world. The world you see and live in everyday is also bombarding you with all the negativity it can, so not only is your positive self fighting against your negative self, it is also fighting against the world.

It's a total mismatch.

It is the positive you in one corner versus the negative you *and* the negative parts of the world in the other.

Is it any wonder people are depressed?

Is it any surprise people are feeling overwhelmed?

If you can understand this, you can begin to see why good people with many blessings still feel down from time to time. You can understand why each day can feel like a burden when it shouldn't. It is almost as if you are under assault from the time you wake until you go to bed. How are you supposed to feel?

In reality, if you are feeling depressed, then that is a completely normal and understandable reaction.

Even so, there is hope. You can fight back and win. It won't be easy. Few things worth having are. But make no mistake, this is war; this is a fight only you can fight and win.

ACTION

CHAPTER 2
THE IMPORTANCE OF ACTION

"Action is the foundational key to all success."
Pablo Picasso

We like to say that a failed action is better than a good thought.

Why do we say this?

Let us explain.

Thoughts generally precede actions and are critical in determining their course, but without an action to bring a thought to life, thoughts are of little use. If this seems like a harsh assessment, it is. However, it's also true.

Another way to say this is thoughts are necessary but insufficient in themselves. It is only after a thought is put into action that it realizes its true potential.

You could also say that not acting on some thoughts is one of the worst indictments against humanity. For instance, if you have an idea that could save lives or help people avoid catastrophe, how could you justify not acting on it? What excuse could possibly exonerate you?

The examples don't need to be extreme. A lifesaving thought could be something as simple as closing a window before a storm or checking if a coffee maker is off. Those thoughts, while seemingly insignificant, could potentially prevent disasters but only if they are acted on.

Action is the lightning bolt that gives a thought life. Action is what makes dreams come true. Action is what brings out the best in us. And on the other side, failing to act on our constructive thoughts has the opposite effect. Failing to act is the worst kind of failure. Failing to act is what brings out the worst in us as human beings. This is why we say a failed action is better than a good thought.

Of course, you must distinguish between constructive and destructive thoughts. We are not saying you should act on a thought for the sake of acting alone. We are saying if you have a thought, which you believe in your heart is a good one, then it is worth taking the risk and acting on it. It is only by putting your thoughts into motion that you will realize your true potential as a human being.

Consider for a moment the difference between a human and ghost. Usually when we think of ghosts, we think of spirits trapped in a place with unfinished business. Ghosts haunt and taunt, but generally their powers in the physical world are limited. Maybe a ghost can flicker a light or shut a door or appear briefly, but normally, ghosts are spirits and as such they have difficulty interacting with much of the physical world. By way of contrast, you exist as a spirit too but are also endowed with the ability to interact physically with the world; however, if you do not act on what your spirit is telling you, then, in a very real sense, you are living like a ghost.

Action is what defines you as a human being. Action brings your spirit to life. Action is what counts. You can have the best ideas in the world but if you don't act on them, then they are of little consequence. Throughout this book, we will be asking you to look at yourself and your thoughts, but of greater significance, we will be calling you to act, to change, and to move. This is why we start talking early about the importance of action.

Think of it this way: When a major motion picture is filmed, you would never hear a director say, "Roll sound. Roll camera. Think!" That would be absurd, wouldn't it? If you think of your life as a movie in production, then without a call to action it's not going to be much of a film to watch. Action truly is the key.

CHAPTER 3
CHANGE YOUR BEHAVIOR AND YOUR THOUGHTS WILL FOLLOW

"If you don't like how things are, change it. You're not a tree."
Jim Rohn

This book stresses action over thought and will make several recommendations to you. And while we sincerely believe we need less thinking and more doing in this world, we also believe it is important to explain our rationale behind this approach. This section will go into that in some detail.

If you've spent time reading self-help books, you'll find that positive thinking is often suggested as a cure for many common problems. It is, according to many, the cure for what ails us. If you've got anxiety, then you need to start thinking positively. If you've been feeling a little down in the dumps, then you need to start thinking positively. If you are under stress or having relationship problems, then you need to start thinking positively.

What exactly is the idea behind positive thinking?

The proponents of positive thinking believe that you feel the way you think, so if you can control your thinking, you can better control your emotions. We also believe in the power of positive thinking because it makes sense and is easy to understand. Thinking positively is practical, logical, and expedient.

But there is a problem.

For all the promise that positive thinking holds, it cannot solve all the problems we are facing, especially those involving our values, deeper beliefs, and ultimate happiness in life. As we see it, positive thinking might help a little, but it can't tell you how to live your life or provide lasting fulfillment. Positive thinking might help you tackle some problems, but it doesn't tell you which problems in life to solve. Positive thinking doesn't tell you what you should do; it is only a self-help tool that leaves your direction in life up to you.

We don't fault positive thinking for its limitations, especially when it comes to finding a path in life or working with deep beliefs. No one should expect positive thinking alone to do that. But more important, our thought processes are unbelievably complex. It would take great skill to coax our deepest thoughts to the surface and properly identify them as culprits of discontent. Pulling thoughts and labeling them might also say more about the person doing the pulling than about the person from whom the thoughts are pulled. And trying to pull your own thoughts would seem as difficult as doing your own surgery.

So where does this leave us?

If positive thinking can only do so much and our deepest thoughts are nearly impossible to isolate and identify, what good is it? What hope is there? We have considered this problem and believe we have a solution. Let's go through it now.

While it might well be true that your thoughts can influence your mood, it is also true they must align with your actions. When your thoughts are not in alignment with your actions or in other words, when what you are thinking doesn't match what you are doing, you experience what is known as cognitive dissonance, which is the unpleasant feeling you get when your thoughts don't match your actions. Using this definition, guilt is a form of cognitive dissonance. For example, you know you shouldn't be stealing something or cheating, but you are doing it anyway. Your thoughts don't match your behavior. You feel guilty and before you know it, you are either thinking it is okay to steal, or you stop stealing because you don't like the way it makes you feel. In short, something has got to give for the behavior to continue.

The most striking thing about cognitive dissonance is it is such an unpleasant state, much like a thorn in your foot, that it can't last for long and at some point, either your actions will pull in line with your thoughts or your thoughts will pull in line with your behavior, but either way the state of dissonance can't last long because it's too uncomfortable.

But instead of being held hostage to our thoughts and a victim to this process, we turn it around and use it to our advantage!

How?

We start engaging in positive behavior right now and let the dissonance process bring our thoughts in line with our new behavior. This way we don't even need to try to guess what our thoughts are; we can change our behavior immediately and know that our thoughts will eventually fall into place. To say it another way, we don't analyze or wait for our thoughts—we change today, this minute! Our thoughts are reluctant bystanders, so we force them where they need to go by changing our behavior.

Now we can't be sure if casinos practice this strategy but what they do fits right in with the theory.

Consider this example.

Let's say you are in Las Vegas with friends, but you don't like gambling or the inside of smoke-filled casinos. However, once you are on the strip, you see one of the casinos is offering an incredible steak and lobster meal for next to nothing.

The casino has not changed your thinking—you still don't like gambling or casinos. But what they have done is offer a deal so good, they are baiting you through the doors.

And by baiting you to go inside, what they have also done is change your behavior—you are now *in* the casino, somewhere you would not normally go.

Now here's the thing:

Once you are inside the casino, your behavior, which is now pro-casino, is out of alignment with your thoughts, which are still anti-casino. Since there is a discrepancy, something has got to give and more than likely, it will be your thoughts. The cognitive dissonance process will start working and before you know it, you will find your thoughts becoming more favorable toward casinos or at least, toward being in one.

Let's take another example:

Let's say you want to start feeling better about yourself in general and decide that one way to do this is by helping others, so you start cleaning out all the things in your house you no longer need and decide to donate them. As you are taking these items to the donation site, a background conversation begins in your mind:

Negative Self (NS): "So we're making some donations?"

Positive Self (PS): "Yes."

NS: "That's really great, but I wonder this stuff actually gets to the people who need it?"

PS: "I'm sure it does."

NS: "I don't know. Sometimes I think it just gets thrown away or sold for drugs."

PS: "I'm sure it will be just fine."

NS: "I hope you know I'm all for you reading those self-help books and all that. You know that, right?"

PS: "Ummm hmmmmm."

NS: "But I'm just wondering how donating a few things is going to make a difference?"

PS: Well, I have to do something. I can't just sit around and do nothing."

NS: "That's true. It just seems a little weak. That's all I'm saying."

PS: "Okay. I got it."

NS: "Are you at least going to get a tax receipt? That way, even if the stuff gets trashed or stolen, it's not a total loss."

Take note that in the dialogue above your negative self is shrewd and knows your weaknesses and exactly where to plant seeds of doubt. It is as if your best friend is sabotaging you.

However, you should also be aware that over time, if the positive behavior persists, then the negative thoughts will eventually modulate and align with the behavior being engaged in.

In short, if you change your behavior, your thoughts will follow. It might not happen immediately, but it will, sooner than later, happen. Using this approach, you don't have to wonder which thoughts are influencing your mood; you can start the behavior you want now, and your thoughts will soon support the new behavior. Positive behavior will lead to positive thoughts more effectively than positive thoughts will lead to positive behavior.

Even if you don't completely agree with this, you must admit that a positive thought will still require an action to be realized, so why would you wait around for the thought to change the behavior when you could begin the positive behavior today? Why not just do the positive behavior and let the dissonance process resolve any conflict?

We hope it is clear now why our focus is on giving directions and encouraging action. Thinking is important, but it can only go so far. Thoughts are elusive and hard to change. Action is immediate and clear.

If you would like to get started on this process right now, you can. In the appendix, we have included a list of positive behaviors you can start doing immediately. Of course, the list is not exhaustive, and there are hundreds of possibilities not listed.

CHAPTER 4
WRITE YOUR TOP THREE GOALS IN LIFE
(And ask the main question: is what you are doing going to lead to them?)

"If you want to live a happy life, tie it to a goal, not to people or things."
Albert Einstein

Now that we've talked about the importance of action, it is time to get focused. Our first recommendation is this: Get in the habit of writing your goals in life and begin making a serious effort to attain them.

We know this is a hard thing to do, but setting goals is a disciplined art. In addition, it is only something you can do. No one can tell you what your goals should be, and no one can know your destination in life—only you can.

Any goal is a good one, but here are some tips for success:

First, whatever goal you set, be sure you can accomplish it in six months or less. We say this because if you set goals that are too far in the future, you risk that they will become detached from your daily life.

Also, if a goal is set too far away, you might stray from it without knowing, and it will do little to help keep you on track. Setting short-term goals helps keep them alive and fresh in your mind.

Second, whatever goal you set, it should be measurable. You should be able to see a goal. It should not be something that exists only as an idea. If someone says his goal is to be "a better person," then that's not measurable.

How would this person know when the goal is accomplished? What does it mean exactly to "be a better person" and how would you know if you became one? Now if this same person set a goal to start doing volunteer work by the end of the month, then that's measurable—that's specific and something you can see.

Third, goals need to be realistic. What is the point of setting a goal you have no chance of reaching? If a freshman in high school says he wants to be an astronaut in three months, how feasible is that? What happens if he does not make it?

If you set goals you have no practical way of meeting, then you also risk getting discouraged. As your coaches, we don't want that to happen.

And remember there is nothing wrong with revising a goal. If you set a goal, and you know you are not going to meet it, we recommend revising it. Goals are for keeping you focused and moving, not making you feel bad. Revising a goal is completely legitimate and nothing to be ashamed of.

Fourth, it is important to break your goals into manageable sections, so you can focus on your progress rather than the outcome. For instance, if you have a goal to write a book, it might be helpful to set your goal as drafting the outline or writing the first chapter versus writing the whole book. In this way, your chances of seeing progress are increased and that will inspire you to keep going.

The purpose of setting goals is not to stress you out or create additional paperwork in your life. The purpose is to keep you on the rails. Time has an awfully funny way of slipping by and without concrete goals you are driving blind, losing time, and never knowing if you are where you really want to be. But if you make realistic short-term goals a routine part of your life, then your life can only get better.

You would never think of going on a hike without knowing the trail, why would you embark on this journey through life with no map for yourself?

Goals are your map and without them, you will get lost. Your goals should be written, kept in your wallet or purse, referred to often, and revised as needed.

When you think of goals, you can think of them in terms of your personal legacy. Your ultimate goals should outlive you and remind others of who you were.

Our final point, and perhaps the most critical one, is the goals you set need to be something you feel passionate about. They should be something you believe in and want to achieve for yourself. The goals we want you to reach are *your* goals. Don't think for a moment you are being selfish. If you choose goals that are important to you individually, then you will be in a better position to help others later. Helping others is another key theme in this book, but for now, for this section, we want you to take the time to set some good goals for yourself.

Goals should lift you up, not bring you down.

CHAPTER 5
SLOW DOWN

"Plenty of people miss their share of happiness, not because they never found it, but because they didn't stop to enjoy it."
William Feather

Our lives are moving faster every day. And the technologies that were supposed to make our lives easier and more socially connected seem to be having the opposite effect. When you go to the mall and see people listening to digital players or toying with their cell phones and blocking out everyone around them, do you have a sense of connection? Do you get the feeling people are happier?

The faster and more connected the world becomes, the more you need to slow things down. When you are rushing and running and trying to get from Point A to Point B as fast as possible, the truth is you are probably missing one of the most important things in life—spending quality time with others.

We are as guilty of this as the next person but how often do we pretend to listen to someone so we can get the conversation over and move on to the next thing we have to do? Like many things we will be talking about in this book, you have to take immediate steps to change this. We don't expect it to change overnight, but we think you should make an effort to slow the pace of everything in your life. And by everything, we mean everything, including your relationships with others.

For instance, the next time someone is telling you a personal story, try to forget you have anything else to do and really concentrate on what the person is saying. Don't think about what you are going to say next—just take a deep breath, slow down, and pay attention.

You should slow the rest of your life too.

The next time you have to go to the store, walk instead of drive. Make the time to take the time and walk slowly through your neighborhood. Look around. Look at the people, the houses, and the plants. Really try to notice and observe. If you go slower, you should begin to see details and things you have been missing. Going fast is great if you are a race car driver, but it is not good when dealing with people or living your life. All these things you are rushing to get to are not more important than the present. Life exists in the moment, not in the past or future. By moving too fast, you are missing some of the best things life has to offer.

A later section of this book deals exclusively with walking. One of the reasons we advocate walking is it forces you to slow down. You will be surprised at how much more you see and feel by moving slower. Take your time. Live in the moment. You can only experience life to the fullest if you slow down.

CHAPTER 6
AT LEAST ONCE EACH DAY, DO SOMETHING YOU ENJOY AND INCLUDE SOMEONE ELSE

"Happy together is better than happy alone."
Kevin Kaohelaulii

Life is way too short to spend it being unhappy and yet that's exactly what many of us are doing—that needs to stop.

In this section, we'd like you to make a list of all the things you like to do. Take your time in doing this and don't rush it. We don't want to set too many conditions, but the things you put on the list should be things you would: a) thoroughly enjoy, b) get you out of the house, and c) involve inviting another person. The last part, inviting another person, is critical because happiness doesn't go far alone.

Think about that for a moment. Think about the times in your life when you have been the happiest. Were you alone or with someone? We would guess you were with someone. So that's why we are asking you to extend an invitation to someone. If they say no, they say no, so you can go ahead by yourself. But if they say yes, that's even better.

We are not saying you can't be happy by yourself; we are saying you can be even happier if you share what you enjoy with someone else. Sharing happiness is the greatest gift you can give someone. We are not asking you to be Mother Teresa—that comes in a later chapter! Here we are asking you to develop a list of all the activities that make you happy, then to share those things with someone. It is as simple as that.

If you are having difficulty thinking of things you would like to do or would like some new ideas, we have put a list of enjoyable activities in the appendix. There is literally no thought required!

All you have to do is select an activity, invite someone along, and do it! And don't worry your thoughts will soon follow.

CHAPTER 7
TAKE TIME TO RELAX EACH DAY

"Relaxation means releasing all concern and tension and letting the natural order of life flow through one's being."
Donald Curtis

Learning how to relax and clear your mind is one of the best things you can do. The problem is it is challenging to find a time and place to do it. Many of us have hectic lives, and it is nearly impossible to make time for ourselves. We have too many commitments and pressures. Even so, this is something we have to make a conscious effort to change.

Think of it this way: Yes, you have a lot to do. Yes, those things are important. And yes, bad things might happen if you don't do all the things you need to do, but what's the point of anything you're doing if it ruins your health and well-being? What is the point of being the world's best employee if you are mentally drained? What is the point of being the world's best parent if you are completely stressed out? What appointment do you have to keep that is more important than your emotional health? Is your life so busy and chaotic that you can't take twenty minutes a day to find a quiet space to relax? Does relaxing for twenty minutes mean you are selfish? If your life is so busy you can't find time to relax, then that's a sign your life is out of control.

Relaxation is at the core of taking care of you. Taking the time to relax is really an acknowledgement that for you to be effective, you need to take care of yourself. We are not asking you to change much here. We are not asking you to join a gym or spa or master meditation. We are only suggesting that you set aside ten to twenty minutes in your day, find a quiet and comfortable spot, and do something you find relaxing.

There are many possibilities. You can read a book, play an instrument, listen to music, nap, or day dream. You can even get a relaxation CD and listen to that.

We can almost guarantee if you start taking the time to relax and do it daily for one month, you will see a big improvement in your mood. In the next section, we will talk about the many forces working against you in this life. If you do not learn how to relax, you will be losing one of the main tools you have for managing the stress caused by obstacles.

You can also think of it this way:

You have to take care of yourself first, so that you can take care of others later. It is just like flight attendants say, "Secure your oxygen mask first and then assist the other person." In other words, if you don't take care of yourself and pass out, how are you going to be able to do anything else?

CHAPTER 8
WALKING

"Slow down and enjoy life. It's not only the scenery you miss by going fast—you also miss the sense of where you are going and why."
Eddie Cantor

We can't find anyone who thinks walking everyday is a bad idea. Walking is to your body as breathing is to your lungs. It's natural. It's positive. It's life.

Walking grounds you. It literally connects you to the earth. If you think about police officers who patrol in cars, what do you notice about them? They are detached and disconnected. Using any kind of transportation other than your legs will detach and disconnect you from the world. If you are not walking, you are passing through the world without fully experiencing it. Police officers who drive through neighborhoods are not experiencing the world. They are experiencing a bubble.

Now contrast this with an officer who is walking a beat. He's not simply passing through in a bubble or on wheels. He is grounded and connected. The officer is experiencing reality as closely as he or she can.

Now think about yourself in a car. Where you might consider driving through a dangerous part of the city, you would never consider walking through certain areas. Why? Because you would be connected. You would be vulnerable. You would be staring reality in the face.

This notion of being connected to the earth and grounded is the most magical thing about walking. When you have your feet on the ground, you can really sense the world and your place in it. Too often we exist inside things and never experience the world. We live *in* houses, drive *in* our cars, and work *in* buildings. We spend entirely too much time indoors—that kind of detachment and estrangement from the world is not healthy or productive.

Walking changes all of that and calms and centers you. Walking forces you to become aware, to observe, to scan, and to participate in the world. Walking helps put things in perspective, helps remind you who you really are, and helps you to see things in a fresh light. If we wanted to push this example to an extreme, crawling is probably the ultimate way to experience reality but that would be a little hard on your hands and knees at this stage of the game!

So far, we've made some key recommendations and hope you will take them to heart. We have recommended writing your top three goals for the next six months, doing something fun with someone else, taking time to relax each day, and now we are recommending walking. We realize we are asking for things that require time on your part but if you want to change your life for the better, you need to stop thinking and start taking action. If it means waking up earlier or staying up later, then do that. If it means giving up something else in your life, then consider that. We are confident these suggestions will work but only if you commit to doing them.

In the next three sections, we will be reviewing the negative elements in our lives and how they affect us. If you follow the positive recommendations we have made so far and begin incorporating them into your life now, then they will be a source of comfort as you work through the next sections.

BASELINE

CHAPTER 9
ADAPTABILITY

"It doesn't matter if the water is cold or warm if you're going to have to wade through it anyway."
Teilhard de Chardin

From time to time, we see someone less fortunate and think, "Gosh, I could never live like that." But the truth is you can handle more than you think you can. You see if there is one thing that defines us as human beings, it is our remarkable ability to adjust and adapt, even in the face of the most adverse situations imaginable. It is in our fundamental nature to adapt to almost anything. If you don't think you could survive in prison, think again. If you don't think you could survive multiple losses, think again. If you don't think you could survive a physical catastrophe, think again. You were built for survival, for adaptation. There is no way around this basic fact of human nature.

With many of us griping about the smallest of life's inconveniences, it is easy to forget just how much we have overcome as a species of survivors. The will to survive and adapt to an ever-changing world is thousands of years old and embedded in our DNA.

Think back on your life and the situations and challenges that have thrown themselves at you. Many times, no doubt, you were put into an unfair situation and were expected to make it work, and you did. You might have doubted yourself at times, but in the end you adapted and survived—you had to.

Think too of all the people around the world, and the situations in which they live from day to day. Think of the slums and the squalor, the droughts and diseases and desolation and right there, right in the middle of it all, sometimes there are people—families, women and children— not only surviving but thriving. How is that possible? How do they keep going?

It is who they are. They are built to adapt and survive.

Okay but where does all this leave us? We are great at surviving. So what? You can say any living thing has two choices: adapt or die.

Now what? Now what ends up happening as a consequence of all this? What is the net result of adaptation?

CHAPTER 10
BASELINES

"Monotony is the law of nature. Look at the monotonous manner in which the sun rises."
 Mohandas Karamchand Gandhi

The result of adaptation is the achievement of a steady state or for want of a simpler term: a baseline. For all the fuss and commotion in our lives, after everything is said and done, after we have finished adjusting, adapting, exploring, and doing everything else we do, at the end of it all, we level out and hit a baseline.

What's even more amazing than that is how fast we can reach a baseline. Just think about this for a moment. Think about how fast you can become bored. How long does it take? Of course, it will depend on what you're doing, but overall, do you get bored quickly? We would venture to guess most people do. Whether it is listening to a lecture or even doing something you normally enjoy, boredom descends as suddenly as a yawn. The time it takes to get bored is the same speed at which you can hit a baseline. It's that fast.

And think of all the things you can get bored with! You can be bored with a book or TV show. You can be bored with school and your job. You can be bored with your life. There are few things in this life that will not bore you at some point.

The phenomenon of baselines is one of the basic aspects of being human, and it stems from our remarkable ability to adapt. We take the unexpected and make it expected. We take the new and make it old. We take the changing and make it unchanging. Whatever life throws at us, ultimately we steady it, level it, and get bored with it. That's just the way it works and dare we say always will. It is part of our universal nature. If there is anything that truly defines the human condition, it is adapting and hitting baselines.

Let's take an example.

Let's say you have been living your whole life in San Diego and have always wanted to live in Boston. You decide the time is right and fly to Boston. Once there, you apply for a few jobs, get lucky, and get offered a job. On returning to San Diego, you pack everything up in a rental truck, say good-bye to all your friends, and give yourself two weeks to get to Boston. The road trip across the country is the adventure of a lifetime. You get to travel through states you never thought you'd see and get to meet all kinds of exciting and new people. Finally, you get to Boston and find a place to rent. The whole experience is a whirlwind. It is exciting *and* stressful, but the excitement trumps any stress.

For the first few weeks, everything is fresh and alive, and it goes on and on like that for weeks and weeks and months and months and maybe even for a year or two, but slowly, as the unfamiliar becomes familiar and the new becomes old, you begin to settle down and find yourself feeling like you've been living there for a long time. Before you know it, you do what you are programmed to do, adapt and hit baseline, and as if by magic, you are back to how you felt in San Diego as if you never left. This isn't strange or weird —it is our nature.

So why are we talking about this?

Because we believe that in order to be truly fulfilled and happy in life, you have to constantly challenge yourself and your established baselines. If you don't, then you may be happy sometimes but not consistently or long-term.

And no matter how great your situation is and how hard you try to put yourself in a good situation, you will hit a baseline at some point and stagnate.

Take a hypothetical example of a sports star. Let's say he has it all and has attained a level of fortune few of us can imagine. He has a loving wife and family, millions in the bank, a legion of adoring fans, and companies begging for his endorsement. But is this enough? Is he happy? Is he fulfilled? No. Amid all his wonderful success and fulfillment, he finds himself bored and lonely. He has, in our view, adapted to his success and hit baseline.

So what does he do?

He tries to mix things up, looks for greener scenery, and begins having affairs. This takes him to a new level of stimulation and makes him happy for a while, but he soon hits a plateau, so he keeps having more and more affairs until it eventually spirals out of control, and his world collapses.

It doesn't matter who you are. Baselines affect us all.

No matter how positive or successful your situation is, you will hit a baseline. Rich or poor, fortunate or not, everyone exists on baselines, unless they make a conscious effort to change. In the star's case, he changed but in a destructive way.

It is our sincerest belief that in order to stay happy in this life, you have to up the ante and keep challenging yourself to do new things, but it has to be done mindfully.

Finding happiness is not as easy as moving from one city to another. It doesn't work like that. Baselines are internal creations, not in the world.

Yes, you may have moved to a positive place. Yes, you may have many successes, but ultimately you will hit a baseline and when that happens, you are going to be right back where you were. And that's why you have to keep challenging yourself.

CHAPTER 11
UP THE ANTE

"The greatest danger for most of us lies not in setting our aim too high and falling short, but in setting our aim too low and achieving our mark."
Michelangelo

We've been talking about baselines for a reason. In our view, the baseline concept helps explain why it is often difficult to stay happy. Look at people who win the lottery or come into an inheritance. When they first get word of the windfall, they are overcome with joy. But what happens after several weeks or months go by? The excitement fades, and reality returns. It is not long before they realize money can't stop the new from becoming old or the unfamiliar from becoming familiar. And if they're not careful, the money is soon gone, and they are literally right back to where they started.

In short, no matter how high you go, you will level out at some point. You have no choice. Rich or poor, we are all programmed to find an equilibrium and steady state.

But it is not all gloom and doom here. Yes, baselines exist and yes, you will always return to them but knowing all this, knowing this process exists, is the first step toward conquering it or at least, keeping it at bay.

The second step is remembering to keep adding things to your life that bring fulfillment.

Let's take the example of Bill Gates. He is a man who created a product nearly everyone with a computer needed and became a billionaire before he turned 32.

Think about what that must be like. Bill Gates is living a life few can imagine. He has fame, fortune, and power. He has a beautiful family, owned a corporation, and employed tens of thousands of people. He is consulted by everyone from Hollywood producers to world leaders. He can do almost anything he wants. If he wants to buy a yacht and sail around the world, he can. If he wants to get in a private jet and fly to Paris for dinner, he can. If he wants to fly to the moon and colonize it, he can.

Yet despite all his fame and power, is he happy? Is he fulfilled? He might be, but it's not due to fame and power.

He is living the life, that's for sure. He can have and do anything he wants. But what has he chosen to do? What is he doing with his life? The last we heard he was trying to rid the world of disease. He is finding fulfillment in helping others.

Now this is pure speculation on our part, but we believe that despite all his power and wealth, Bill Gates is like the rest of us. But, in his case, he seems to have figured out that in order to stay fulfilled in this life, he had to get beyond himself and challenge himself to do great things. In short, he had to *up the ante*. He seems to understand he has to keep challenging himself to do more to help people and change lives for the better. His legacy is creating a better world.

We hope that Bill Gates doesn't see any of what he is doing as a burden. We hope he is enjoying the challenges and beating his personal best. And we hope he is as happy as he can possibly be.

What's interesting to us is there is little difference between Bill Gates and our sports celebrity. Both have achieved a remarkable level of success, personally and professionally, and both have hit baselines. However, and this is the difference, one chose to ante up, the other down. One found the key; the other is still searching.

You cannot find true happiness keeping things as they are, but you also have to change in the right direction. You have to push yourself to do more than you are doing now, but it has to be something that involves helping others, something significant. It has to be beyond you. And while we don't know how fast you will hit your next baseline, you can rest assured you will, so you can't stop pushing yourself to do more in the biggest way you can.

The best way we can think of to do this is to tie these baseline challenges to the goals you set. Your goals, in this way, become your path to sustained happiness. Not all of your goals have to be lofty but maybe one or two can be. Up the ante and tie it to your goals—that's the single best advice we can give.

BOMBARDMENT

CHAPTER 12
UNDER BOMBARDMENT

"For most folks, no news is good news; for the press, good news is not news."
Gloria Borger

In the opening section of this book, we make the claim the world is a negative place and for some that might seem like a rash assertion. We should clarify that we are not referring to the earth itself but rather to ourselves as its inhabitants. As much as we love people, humanity itself is the greatest source of negativity. You only have to stroll through a prison yard or get stuck in grid-lock traffic to feel the negativity we are talking about.

Of course, we realize we are including ourselves in this indictment and don't want to incriminate ourselves too much, but it is a tough world out there, and we aren't making it any better. Life is rough, and people make it rougher.

We still believe change is possible but only if we take meaningful actions to change. We try to stay optimistic but also need to be true to what we see in the real world. We can't sit here and tell you the world is an entirely happy place because that, quite honestly, has not been our experience.

To complicate matters, the media make things many times worse by rubbing our faces in gruesome stories night after night. And as technology expands, so does the media and its reach.

And if you can agree with us on that point, then it isn't much further to acknowledge we live under a barrage of negativity from the minute we wake until the time we go to sleep. It comes from every television, every radio, and every newspaper.

If you don't believe us, try this:

Go get your local paper and count the number of negative articles compared to the positive. Which one is higher?

Sadly, that's what sells.

Not only are you being bombarded from the media, many people around you, including yourself, aren't helping and are often repeating what they hear from the news.

You are trapped on a ride you can't get off.

If you are besieged with negativity from nearly everyone and everything, is it any wonder you might be feeling negative too?

What's even more surprising is after having been under attack for years and years, it begins to feel normal. It begins to feel familiar, then comfortable, then before you know it, you are not only unaware of how much negative energy you are absorbing, you might actually come to find it comforting. Misery becomes your pillow. Do you see how twisted things have become when we find enjoyment in watching someone else in misery on television?

But we believe you know, deep down, this is not how it should be. We know you know this isn't good for you.

Negative news brings you down, bums you out, and though it might make you feel better for a time, it eventually wears you down and sucks the life straight out of you.

Floating in a sea of garbage might feel right after a while, but it surely isn't good for you.

We don't want to harp on this issue of how much negativity there is in the world. We only want you to acknowledge and be aware of it.

Denying it won't make it go away.

CHAPTER 13
STOP OR LIMIT ALL NEWS MEDIA

"I do not take a single newspaper, nor read one a month, and I feel myself infinitely happier for it."
Thomas Jefferson

It is amazing to us that Thomas Jefferson, who died in 1826, wrote the above quote. What is that saying to us? It says that in 150 years things haven't changed much. The world is still a tough place, and the news is still throwing all the negativity it can at you.

For now, we hope you can agree and acknowledge that there is too much negativity in the world and that you must take steps to manage it. And this leads us to our current suggestion, which is to stop or limit the media in your life. By media, we mean radio, television, print, and internet communication.

Are we suggesting a complete news blackout? Not quite. We realize it might not be realistic or practical to stop all the media you are coming into contact with, so if you can't turn it off or control it, then by all means limit it and choose positive news to read and focus on.

If you are addicted to the news, then try cutting your exposure in half. For instance, if you listen to talk radio three hours a day, cut it to an hour and a half. You don't have to stop instantly or insulate yourself from reality, but you need to make a conscious effort to pull back from it.

We venture to guess if you at least cut back, you will begin to feel better for it.

Think about it.

A young girl is molested, or a priest is murdered, or twelve people die in an accident, how does it benefit you to know these things?

How will knowing these horrible things change your life? What can you do to change these things?

In short, you need to cut back on all the news. It isn't helping you and isn't meant to. The news exists to make money and get you to buy something from one of their sponsors. And worse, they know what you like. They know you and are manipulating you. The news, in that sense, is really no different from tobacco companies.

They are trying to get you hooked on what is essentially a deadly product, and they know that once they've got you hooked, it is a tough addiction to break. The good thing is you can quit. You need to start small and gradually cut back until you are completely weaned. It worked for Thomas Jefferson; it can work for you.

NEGATIVE

CHAPTER 14
WHAT IS NEGATIVE?

"Battle not with monsters lest you become one."
Friedrich Nietzsche

Before we begin this section, we want to make it clear that while there is a lot of negativity in the world and in ourselves, we do not want to dwell on this fact. We believe dwelling on the negative only gives it more power, so that's not what we want to do. What we want to do is address it and move on. We also believe we would be less than honest if we tried to act as if there were no negativity in the world. In our view, there is simply too much toxicity in the world to ignore.

We have been using the word "negative" without defining it but now would like to. The purpose of defining what is negative is not to turn this into a book of rules but to give you a general definition you can use in your life.

We define negative as:

Anything that makes you (or somebody else) feel bad or has adverse effects.

In developing this definition, we realize there will never be a perfect definition that satisfies all possible situations. The truth is we do not need and are not looking for one. We are only trying to convey a concept. We believe the definition is clear, but there is always room for interpretation.

For example, in talking about what is negative, someone could say, "Well you know I stopped taking my blood pressure medication because it made me feel bad and two weeks later, I had a stroke, so wow, your definition isn't very good." In a case like this, we would have to say this person needs to go back and read the definition more carefully. The definition of negative is anything that makes you feel bad *or* has adverse effects. In the above example, the result was an adverse effect, so, in the end, it was still a negative thing to do.

CHAPTER 15
DRAWN TO THE NEGATIVE

"Man is fond of counting his troubles, but he does not count his joys."
Fyodor Dostoevsky

The next trait we'd like to discuss is something that appears to be uniquely human and that is what might be called an "attraction to the negative." And again, by negative, we mean anything that makes you feel bad or has adverse effects.

Let's start with a simple example.

Let's say your friend has decided to paint a room and has been working on it all day. You stop by, and he tells you he has just finished. You walk in, and the room looks great, a big improvement over what it had been. But as you look over the room, your attention is drawn to a spot on the wall that appears to have been missed. It doesn't matter 99.9999% of the room is perfectly painted. You are pulled, almost inexplicably, to the little spot he missed and not only that, you don't hesitate to mention it. Now why is that? What compels us to do things like that?

Let's take another example.

You are driving down the freeway and suddenly encounter a traffic jam. From your vantage point, you can see down the road a mile and notice there are flashing lights and emergency vehicles. There has been an accident, but it is on the other side of the freeway. There is nothing obstructing traffic on your side of the freeway other than people slowing to look at what has happened. Your first thought is, "Geesh, these people should get a life and quit being looky loos." But as you inch forward, you feel yourself drawn to look too. Perhaps drawn isn't even the right word—it is more like compelled. You feel yourself compelled to look over. You know it can't be good. You suspect people have been hurt or killed or at least cars wrecked. You know it is none of your business, but you make it your business and sneak a parting glance. When you get wherever you are going, you also report what you saw to anyone who will listen. Why is that? Why did you feel compelled to look at the accident?

We don't need to speculate on why we are drawn to the negative. We just know everyone is. For our purposes, however, it is important we bring up this tendency, so we are aware of it.

Can you see what you are up against? Not only are you fighting against all the negativity in the world and in you, you are attracted and drawn to it. It is a fatal human flaw. The pull of the negative should not be underestimated and is not something you or anyone else can change.

You need to know that while you might not be able to fully control this tendency, awareness can lead to increased control.

CHAPTER 16
CREATING A LIST OF NEGATIVE FORCES IN YOUR LIFE

"The greatest happiness is to know the source of unhappiness."
Fyodor Dostoyevsky

We should let you know we are not only writing this book but are living it too. We didn't see how we could write a book like this without practicing what we preach. As a result, we have to say this next recommendation turned out to be one of the most surprising.

First, we thought that because there is so much negativity in the world, it would be easy to write down a list of all the negative forces in our lives, but surprisingly, we struggled and that was not what we expected. It was easy to identify a few big ticket items like too much television and fast food, but after that, it became more difficult. It became a challenge to do an honest assessment and start labeling things as negative. The definition helps, but it is still harder than you might think to do a self-appraisal.

Second, in creating the list, the biggest shock of all was the realization that the greatest negative influence in our lives was not an outside force but an inside one—*ourselves*! That's right. Our final lists included ourselves as negative forces in our lives. What a wake-up call that turned out to be!

The truth is we are often the biggest negative influence in our own lives. Now don't take this too far. We don't want to be blaming ourselves for everything, but the reality is we often excel at making ourselves feel bad.

And what's more, you are always with you. You are with yourself 24 hours a day, 7 days a week, 365 days per year, rain or shine. You are always there and can often criticize yourself into depression.

In fact, you are your own resident expert in making yourself feel bad.

Don't freak about this but if you end up putting yourself on the list, that's totally acceptable. We did.

And if you think about it, it makes sense because you are your worst enemy most of the time.

The world might be a negative place, but you play a bigger role in it than you think and if you are making yourself feel bad, then you need to be aware of that and take action.

The first step is awareness; the second is doing something to control and better manage the negative forces you identify.

CHAPTER 17
MANAGE AND CONTROL ALL THE NEGATIVE FORCES IN YOUR LIFE

"It is easier to stay out than get out."
Mark Twain

Now you have your list of negative forces, what do you make of it? Have you put yourself on the list? Did any other people make the list? Are the things or people on the list things you can limit or get away from? Is there anything missing from the list that you might have conveniently overlooked?

On our lists, all the items posed challenges and required us to assess how committed we were to changing our lives for the better.

Let's take an example.

Fast food. We know it is not good for us and is making us fat and putting us at risk for disease. And yet we struggle everyday to avoid it. Every single day it crosses our minds. It is hard to ignore because there are fast-food places on nearly every corner and city block. It is constantly in our faces, constantly on our minds, and constantly calling us. And we know, clear as day, none of that stuff is good for us, none of it. It is another form of bombardment, only you can smell and taste it too!

And so now fast food sits on our list as a big fat negative. At times, it even seems to be mocking us from the list itself and saying, "So I'm on your list. What are you going to do about it?" And that really is the question. What are we going to do? (We should also note fast food made the list not because it made us feel bad but because we know it is having adverse effects on our health.)

Our first strategy, and the one we recommend, is not to screech to a stop or try to immediately eliminate all the negatives at once. If you can, then that's great, and you should do that, but we are not sure that's the most effective approach.

We like the approach of gradually pulling back and limiting your consumption until it is down to such a small amount it will be easy to give up.

For instance, let's say you are going into a coffee house everyday and buying a fancy sweet drink. You could keep doing that but start switching to nonfat milk. You'll notice it doesn't taste the same, but you won't be giving up that much. Then, the following week or so, you switch to a nonsweetened or regular coffee drink. You'll definitely notice the change but then again you're still getting a treat! Then once you make it through that, start skipping a day, then another, and another, and another, until you only go to the coffee house for special occasions or as a reward for something good you did.

We do not want you to stress yourself out or feel like you are depriving yourself of guilty pleasures. In fact, if you start feeling that way, then you have gone too far too fast and need to start over. None of these recommendations should ever feel like a burden. You should feel good about doing them or hold off on doing them until you can.

Our strongest recommendation is you cut back on the negative influences gradually.

You let the negative influences into your life for a reason, and they must be serving some purpose, or you would have already let them go. If you try to fight too hard against them, then they will only return, maybe even stronger, so go slow.

With the negative people in your life, it might be more challenging because you cannot necessarily control your time with them, especially if it is a work setting. But you can control how much "mind time" you give them, so the same principle would apply—cut back gradually until their influence on your life is minimal. Once you hit that point, it will be much easier to let go completely and feel good about it.

We also want to point out that we are not saying to "throw the baby out with the bath water." Everyone you know is bound to make you feel bad at some time or other, so cutting out negative people should be the exception, not the rule. When dealing with others, some tolerance and patience will still be needed. We discuss this issue in more detail later in the book.

If you happened to list yourself as a negative force in your life, then that will be perhaps the biggest challenge of all. It is pretty difficult to cut back on yourself! However, you can learn how to better manage your negative tendencies, and we delve into that more in some later sections, so please keep going. You are on the right track!

CHAPTER 18
IDENTIFY THREE AREAS FOR PERSONAL IMPROVEMENT AND START WORKING ON THEM

"A habit cannot be tossed out the window; it must be coaxed down the stairs a step at a time."
 Mark Twain

Now you've got a list of the negative forces in your life, we are going to take a chance and say that even if you didn't put yourself on the list, there is still room for improvement in your life and in how you relate to others. But you should also know it is hard to look at yourself and see yourself as others do. You might even say it is an impossibility to have a point of view on your point of view. After all, if you were looking at yourself from a different perspective, then that perspective would become your new point of view, and it again would be hard for you to see yourself from the outside looking in.

Therefore, in order for you to get a better perspective on any areas where you might be able to improve, you are going to need someone else's perspective. Ideally, it should be somebody you trust and somebody whose opinion is not going to devastate you. If you ask the wrong person, it could backfire and lead to problems.

Here's the recommendation:

Find someone you trust and who knows you well and ask them to write down three things about you that they like. It can be anything about you. There is no restriction on what it can be.

You also need to ask them to write down three things about you that bother them. It can be almost anything about you, *but it has to be something that you can change*. Be sure to tell them to take their time and to write the list when you are not around. When they finish the list, simply have them give it to you.

You can also turn this into a relationship-building exercise by asking them if they want you to make a list for them.

We're hoping the person you ask, perhaps your spouse or close friend, will be fair and won't turn this into a payback opportunity.

We sincerely believe the feedback you get from someone else will be more useful than the feedback you will get from yourself. And as painful and anxiety-provoking as this recommendation is, we believe it can only make you better.

At the end of it all, by doing this suggestion you are stepping up and becoming "the bigger person." There is absolutely nothing wrong in asking for feedback about yourself from someone you have in your life. If you can't ask someone for honest feedback, or they aren't willing to give it to you, then perhaps that is a sign of a deeper problem.

Once you have the feedback, you can talk with the person about it and see if there is more information that would be helpful to know. And after that is clarified, then you need to develop a plan for addressing the issues.

It will be interesting to see if the things they told you were things you already suspected or if they were a revelation. If they confirmed your suspicions, then that suggests you might be able to trust your self-assessments. If they are new things, then perhaps this exercise is something you should do from time to time with those in your life who are important to you.

Keep the list in a safe place and refer to it often. As you start to address the problems on the list, it will also be worth seeing if you notice any improvement in your relationships.

CHAPTER 19
USE NEGATIVE EMOTIONS AS SIGNS YOU HAVE DRIFTED OFF COURSE

"A pessimist is one who makes difficulties of his opportunities and an optimist is one who makes opportunities of his difficulties."
Harry Truman

It is hard to believe painful emotions have any positive value. We are told anger leads to heart problems, and depression weakens our immune system, so what could possibly be positive about negative emotions? What is the upside?

Pay attention to your feelings and listen to them but don't dwell on them, especially if they're negative. There are some emotions such as grief that are perfectly natural and are not telling you anything other than the obvious. Sometimes, emotions are simply a part of living.

For us, negative emotional states like anger, resentment, depression, and irritability all serve a key beneficial purpose.

Negative emotions are signals you are drifting off course with your life and need to get your actions and thoughts back on track. You can look at them as flashing red lights telling you that you are too close to the edge of the road. You can also think of them as a good friend calling you back to a trail in the woods. If you can see these emotions this way, then they are not harmful at all and serve a vital purpose in helping you.

If you find yourself feeling depressed, then you should know your thinking has strayed from positive to negative, and you need to take positive actions to reset things. If you are feeling angry or like you are going to explode, then you can know your thinking has become extreme and so will your actions. And if you find yourself irritated, you can know your thinking has closed in on you and is controlling you instead of you controlling it.

Negative emotions are *calls to action.* They are telling you something, warning you, pleading with you, begging you to get back over to positive action and thinking.

If you can begin to see negative emotions as the key to staying positive, you will truly be on the way toward changing your life.

It is a near certainty you will continue to feel negative emotions, but you don't see them as something to get rid of. See them for what they are— signals and markers you have strayed from where you need to be physically and mentally. And in this sense, we could not survive without painful emotions any more than society could function without a police force or someone keeping us in check. Negative emotions are unpleasant, but they serve as referees letting you know things are out of bounds.

POSITIVE

CHAPTER 20
WHAT IS POSITIVE?

"Pessimism leads to weakness, optimism to power."
William James

You might have found it a little surprising a book about staying happy has spent so much time talking about negativity, and the role everyone plays in it. In writing this book, we struggled with how much negativity to talk about, but in the end, we felt there was no way to avoid it. But now, if you've made it this far, you've reached a turning point. Now we've addressed the negative and talked about how to deal with it to some extent, the goal is to move on and upward with the positive. Yes, finally, we are going to start talking about the brighter side of things. That's not to say we can stop talking about the negative, but as much as we can, we will try to keep things as positive as possible.

As you might expect, the definition of what is positive is pretty much the opposite of what defines the negative. And again, while there is no one perfect definition, this is our attempt at it:

Positive is anything that makes you feel good and has no significant negative effects.

You might have noticed our definitions of positive and negative are based on how something makes you feel. We believe this is important because emotions can be a guide when all else fails. For instance, if somebody at work leaves you feeling stupid after you ask a simple question, then that's significant. Feelings might not always be based on facts, and you might be the only one having the feelings but that doesn't lessen their influence. You are having your feelings for a reason and should be mindful of what they are telling you. For that reason, how something makes you feel is the centerpiece of our definitions.

Also, in talking about what is positive, you can do things that make you feel good but aren't good for you. That's why we extended the definition to include the provision "*and* has no significant negative effects." For instance, eating a cheese burger can make you feel great, but over time, it can have significant negative effects on your health and for that reason, we would not see it as positive.

Now are we saying you can never eat a cheese burger? Of course not! That's not reasonable.

Eating whatever you want every now and then should not be a problem because that's probably not going to harm you. But eating fast food every single day is another story and probably would.

In summary, positive is anything that makes you feel good, makes you feel warm, makes you hopeful, and raises you up *and* is not bad for you. Negative is anything that makes you feel bad, gloomy, and down *or* is bad for you. There will never be perfect definitions that cover every possible situation, but these definitions are simple and easy to remember and should cover the majority of situations you might find yourself in.

CHAPTER 21
CREATE A LIST OF THE POSITIVE FORCES

"Reflect upon your present blessings of which every man has many-not on your past misfortunes, of which all men have some."
Charles Dickens

You have heard at one time or another that you should be grateful for what you have and should count your blessings. And depending on the situation and how you were feeling at the time, you could have responded in any number of ways. You might have said, "Yeah, right" in a sarcastic voice, or you might have thought about it for a moment and realized it was a valid point.

It seems we have a knack for conveniently overlooking things that are going well in our lives. In the previous sections, we've speculated on why we think that is, so there's no point belaboring that.

It is hard to appreciate all the blessings you do have in your life, especially when things might not be going well.

When things are not going well, often the last thing you want to hear is someone telling you to count your blessings and write them down.

But guess what? That's exactly what we are going to tell you to do. We are not calling them blessings; we call them "positive forces." We call them that because they can be literally anything in your life that meets the definition of positive and that could be a number of things. It could be a perfume, a poem, or a person. It could be a book, a bath, or a beach. It is anything that makes you feel good and is not bad for you.

So why are we asking you to write another list?

First, we want you to think about what is positive in your life and bring it to the top of your consciousness. We want you to scrutinize your life and everything in it and clearly identify the good influences. The act of writing helps the process.

Second, once you have it written, seeing the words will help solidify it your mind and keep it in your awareness and that's exactly what we want. Remember how we said dwelling on the negative gives it more power. It's the same concept. Dwelling on the positive gives it more power and again, that's what we want. Writing encourages dwelling and in this case, that's a good thing.

Our strategy here is basic. We want you to identify the positive things in your life *and* increase them.

And coming from the other direction, we want you to identify the negative things in your life *and* decrease them.

Increase the positive, decrease the negative—it is as simple as that.

But if you don't have a list of what's positive and negative, it is easy to forget what they are and maintain the status quo, which we have already determined isn't what we want to do.

So when you get a chance, take out a piece of paper, get a pen, and start writing the positive influences in your life. Hopefully, the list will be longer than the negative list you did a few sections ago.

And don't forget you can put yourself on the list too!

CHAPTER 22
VISUALIZE YOUR PERFECT SELF

"Perfection is attained by slow degrees; it requires the hand of time."
Voltaire

A common problem that leads to trouble is how we define ourselves and inevitably, we do it by comparing ourselves to others. That's not far from how real estate agents determine the value of houses—they compare what the last house on the block sold for and use that to gauge the value of yours. When it comes to people, it seems nearly impossible not to compare ourselves to each other. Comparative analysis is what we do. It is yet another thing deep in our nature.

But when we compare ourselves to others is that helpful and giving us useful information?

When we took introductory psychology a while ago, we were told there were many ways to define ourselves.

One way is to compare yourself to what most people are doing and if you are doing what they are, then you are okay. But is that true? For instance, many people have cavities but is that a good thing?

Another way to define yourself is to compare yourself to an ideal type of person like Mother Teresa or Abraham Lincoln but using that approach most of us would probably fall short.

So where does that leave us? If we are destined to compare ourselves to something, what should it be? What should be our guide?

We have considered this problem and believe one solution is to imagine your ideal or perfect self and compare yourself to that. In fact, we would even suggest you not only get a clear vision of your ideal self, but you begin to imagine yourself as that person.

We want you to get in the habit of trying to imagine what the perfect you would be like. How would he or she act? What would your ideal self consider important in this world? What would your perfect self be doing that you are not doing now?

We understand it might take some time before you can get the image of your ideal self clear in your mind and that it takes practice. You should also know if you cannot visualize your perfect self, and you find yourself drawing a blank, then that only means it is something you need to work on. It doesn't mean you can't do this.

Once you get an image clear in your mind of what your ideal self is, then you need to start believing you are that person and tell yourself:

"There is no difference between my ideal self and me. We are one and the same, now and forever."

We realize this might seem awkward at first, but it is much better than the alternative, which is continuing to compare yourself to others.

Comparing yourself to others is a dead end because you will never be them, and they will never be you. There is only one you and that's who you should be comparing yourself to!

CHAPTER 23
EXPERIENCE ONE INSPIRATIONAL THING A DAY

"We cannot always control our thoughts, but we can control our words, and repetition impresses the subconscious, and we are then the master of the situation."
Florence Scovel Shinn

We understand we are asking you to do many new things, but we don't believe there is any way for you to change without taking action. On the back cover of the book, we have included a checklist to help you keep track of the things we are asking you to do on a daily basis, but we would also like to make a quick point.

None of the things we are asking you to do should feel like a burden. If they do, then you need to pause for a moment and consider what we've been asking you to do. So far, we've asked you to set three goals, relax, walk, and do things you enjoy with others. We have also asked you to set goals for personal improvement and cut back on the news. Should these things feel like a burden or chore? We certainly hope not. We understand you might not be used to getting so many suggestions but other than that these should all be things you might have been doing already. In short, there really is no reason why you can't do most of these things. We know you can, so make a commitment and keep going.

With that said, we would like to introduce our next recommendation:

Experience one inspirational thing a day.

What do we mean by this?

We want you to get inspired and find something in your life that makes you feel excited. Everyone is different, so what works for us might not work for you. We want you to do or experience *anything* that inspires you at least once every single day.

If it is reading scriptures, do that. If it is watching a scene from a movie or listening to a song, do that. If it is exercising or running, do that. If it is looking at a family photo or saying a positive affirmation, do that. The key is you must do it daily, *and* it must be something inspiring. We want inspiration, not stagnation!

This might date us a little but if you think of how you felt the first time you saw the montage of Rocky Balboa working out in the original *Rocky* movie, then that's the feeling we want you to have. If you haven't seen the movie, rent it.

If you have seen the movie, do you remember how that scene made you feel? Can you remember the theme song? It might sound a little corny but that's the level of inspiration we want you to strive for every day.

You don't have to spend much time; a few minutes each day should work.

CHAPTER 24
DO NICE LITTLE THINGS

"You will never change your life until you change something you do daily."
Mike Murdock

If you've read from the beginning of the book to here, we'd like to believe you are well on your way toward a happier and more fulfilling life. We've made some key recommendations so far, and we hope you are following through with each one. We really believe if you were to stop reading this book right now and did no more than what we've recommended so far, you would still notice an improvement in your life. But here's the exciting news:

We are just getting started, and there is much more to come! We've made a few scratches and dents but still have a lot more to offer and suggest.

That said, if you are following along with the recommendations and doing them faithfully, we believe you are already changing and putting out more positive energy, and now you can start doing nice little things for others.

We believe if you are to attain true happiness in life, then it is essential you start reaching out to more people. We have already recommended that you do this with enjoyable activities. Now we are recommending you start doing nice things for two or three people you encounter each day but not limit it to an enjoyable activity. We want you to reach out to others and do two to three small and selfless acts each day.

We are not asking you do anything dramatic. It could be something as simple as saying "Hello" to someone you normally wouldn't or opening a door for someone. It could be walking over to someone at work you usually pass and making small talk for a minute. It could be sharing a snack with a coworker or asking someone if they need help carrying some packages.

The gist of this is that now you are becoming more positive yourself, you need to extend yourself to others in small but significant ways. The persona you project is changing, and how others perceive you will also change. You are not the same person you were yesterday. You are becoming a better person, and the world needs you to show it. People will not know how nice you really are if they can't see it. You have to make just a little effort to show them, and they will catch on quick.

Remember it doesn't have to be anything big. You just need to make the effort. The smallest gesture will work, and it will not only have an influence on you, it will have a big effect on others. Think of how you feel when you're staying at a hotel, and the maid leaves a mint on your pillow. It is a small gesture but doesn't it go a long way? It is the same concept, only applied to your daily life.

If you are having trouble coming up with ideas for nice little things to do, we have included a partial list of possibilities in the appendix. The list is not exhaustive and is only meant to get you going. We would encourage you to be creative and come up with your own list of ideas.

CHAPTER 25
JOURNALING THE POSITIVE

"Writing crystallizes thought and thought produces action."
Paul J. Meyer

We realize the idea of creating a journal is nothing new, but of all the recommendations we are making, this is probably one of the most difficult to follow. There are reasons for this. For one, doing a journal requires discipline and conviction. It requires you to study your life and take the time to extract the positive. But here's the thing—those things we mention as "difficult" are actually the most important qualities we want to develop in you.

Let us explain.

If you were to consistently follow through with every recommendation we made in this book, then that would be a good sign you are sincere about turning your life around. It would also mean you were serious about not only challenging the negative parts of yourself but also the negativity in the world. And not only challenging them but pushing them back and turning yourself into a force for the greater good.

What does it take to do something like that? What does it take to turn something negative into something positive? What does it take to stay hopeful when much around you isn't? In our mind, it takes discipline and conviction. In other words, the same qualities that are needed to change you as a person are the same qualities it takes to create a journal.

It is remarkable how we often associate the qualities—discipline and conviction—with some grand undertaking like carving Mount Rushmore or becoming a black belt in karate, but those very same elements are also needed for smaller activities. Things as simple as building a model or creating a piece of furniture or even writing a small book all require those qualities. So in recommending that you begin creating a journal, we are cultivating discipline and conviction in you.

We would like to mention that when we say *journal* we are not saying you have to write something. You could also do an audio or video recording, but our best advice is to write in a journal daily or at a minimum, three times per week.

What you journal about is entirely up to you, but it should be about something positive that has recently happened to you. Anything that made you happy or brought a smile to your face or inspired you would be appropriate. The journal is not for venting or ranting. It is about reflecting on your day-to-day life and recording the positive things you remember.

As we said in the beginning, this is one of the more difficult things we are asking you to do, but it is one of the suggestions that will strengthen the qualities you need to succeed and help you remember the positives on days that are difficult.

CHAPTER 26
FOSTERING A POSITIVE, PERSONAL ENVIRONMENT

"Write your injuries in dust, your benefits in marble. "
Benjamin Franklin

As humans, our senses are incredibly important. Without them, we would be lost. Outside intuition and other strictly cognitive processes, everything we know about the world comes to us through our senses. And we have already established we live in a world where we are bombarded with negativity. This bombardment is not without an effect on us. If you are bombarded with radiation, doesn't that have a long-term effect on your DNA? If you are bombarded with loud music, doesn't that affect your hearing? If you are engulfed in smoke, won't that affect your sense of smell? So doesn't it stand to reason that being bombarded with negativity would have a long-term effect on your mind? In our opinion, it absolutely would. And the longer it goes on, the greater the effect, so if this has been going on since you were born, it doesn't take much imagination to guess how severely affected you might be by now.

So where does this leave us?

It leaves us with the recommendation we are proposing to you now: You need to make a conscious effort to create *more* positive stimulation around you.

You need to start posting positive sayings where you live and work. You need to listen to soothing music. You need to hang up pictures on the wall that inspire and motivate and make you feel good. Get rid of clutter and tidy the disarray around you. Get cinnamon sticks and boil them and let the smell take over your home. You need to do anything and everything you can to turn your environment from negative to positive.

You might not have control of the world, but you do have control over your living space. Take control of it and make it a shrine to calming energy. Think of your living or working spaces as places you can go to get recharged. Think of your living and working spaces as welcoming and comforting places.

The world you see embeds itself in your mind. If your personal spaces are cramped, cluttered, and unpleasant, all of that gets embedded in your mind. If your spaces are clean and comforting, then that gets embedded. Which way do you want it to be?

CHAPTER 27
POSITIVE DREAM PROGRAMMING

"Judge of your natural character by what you do in your dreams."
Ralph Waldo Emerson

One of the most curious facts about us is how much time we spend sleeping. There are many ideas about why we sleep, but nobody knows for sure. One thing is for sure though and that is we need to sleep and if we don't, we suffer.

Taking a middle-of-the-road estimate, we spend about one third of our lives sleeping. If you think about that, that's astounding. One third of what we call living, *one third*, is spent not really "living" but sleeping. Sleeping must be fairly important to our overall well-being if we have to spend one third of our lives doing it.

With so much of our lives devoted to sleeping, is there any potential opportunity we are missing? Is there some way we could use that time to help us become more productive and positive? Possibly.

Think about it like this:

The mind is always on and running, even if the body isn't. The mind is also susceptible to suggestions and has a strong tendency to process whatever it has most recently experienced. Taking these together, we believe it is entirely possible to influence your dreams by telling yourself what you want to dream about right before you drift off to sleep.

Of course, we haven't funded a study to prove this, but we have found it to be true from our own experiences. From our experience, here are the keys to making it work:

1) You have to say out loud what you want to dream about.

2) You have to repeat it at least 7-10 times. (The more the better)

3) The instructions have to be directive. For example, "I am going to dream about walking on the beach tonight."

4) You have to say it right before you are getting ready to fall asleep.

Now we understand this might seem strange at first but think about how much time you spend sleeping and how much of that time you could channel into something productive. Shouldn't you have a say in what your dreams are about? What harm could trying possibly cause? In our opinion, none.

There are mental processes at work we might never understand but that doesn't mean we can't try to harness those processes for our benefit.

Positive dream programming is one of those things you don't hear a lot about but that doesn't mean it's not possible or a good thing to try.

PEOPLE

CHAPTER 28
IT IS ALL ABOUT RELATIONSHIPS

"Man is a knot into which relationships are tied."
Antoine de Saint-Exupery

Of all the quotes in this book, this is one of our favorites. It brings up perhaps the biggest thing about the nature of human existence, which is this:

We are social creatures and cannot live without each other.

This fact is not only true for human beings but other species as well.

Strangely, this powerful truth is conveniently brushed aside once we become teenagers. We get too wrapped up, especially in Western culture, in our ego and independence. We start thinking we don't need anyone for anything and can make it on our own. And we get pretty convinced of it all.

But like most truths, this one is awfully hard to keep denying. Try as we might to be happy alone, we are probably the happiest when we are with others.

Think about the happiest times in your life. Were you by yourself or with someone?

Our guess is you were with someone.

Think about people who have gone off and lived by themselves. What were their lives like? What were they like? How did their stories end? Do you get a positive image in your mind when you think of someone who lives in complete isolation? We think of Tom Hanks in the movie *Castaway*. If you haven't seen the movie, he was stranded on a tropical island and nearly went insane but kept it together by befriending a volleyball named Wilson.

The strange thing about people is they often seem to be a double-edge sword. On the one hand, we know we need each other to experience true happiness, but on the other, you also run the risk of getting hurt by letting people into your life.

It is a dilemma.

You can almost say you can't live with or without people. But the truth is you absolutely need people in your life and whether others want to admit it or not, they need you too, yet we often walk around in our bubbles acting like we don't need anyone for anything.

We need each other. Make no mistake about it.

Looking back at our collective history, it is only by banding together we survived as a species. Being together is in our DNA. And though science and technology are changing this, we still need each other to keep our species going.

We cannot escape people and shouldn't try to. Trying to get people out of your life would be like trying to get yourself out of your life. It is impossible. In fact, you *are* people. When looking in the mirror you might see yourself as an all-powerful individual who is different from everyone else but when you are walking down a crowded street and someone else is looking at you, you are lost in the crowd.

We are not saying you should never have time alone, or you need hundreds of friends and social activities to be happy. We are saying life is all about people. Happiness is all about people.

People are the inescapable reality of this whole thing we call living life. And at the end of it all, at the very end of everything, if you can't get along with people, you won't be happy. Other people are like a mirror—they reflect your humanity and without them, you can't have any sense of who you really are. As much as you might say people are driving you crazy, the truth is you will go crazy without people in your life.

The key to happiness comes down to others and helping them. And in the end, helping each other is what we are all about; it is the basis of our humanity and ultimately, our greatest fulfillment in life.

CHAPTER 29
BE MINDFUL OF HOW YOU VIEW OTHERS

"Are you really sure that a floor can't also be a ceiling?"
M.C. Escher

By now, we hope we have established why people are important and why you need to involve them in your life. But of course, things are not that simple. If they were, everybody would be happy and most certainly, that's not the case. Happiness, as you might be realizing, takes work to achieve. You can't stop moving if you are to stay happy. Remember the baseline?

Perhaps one of the most remarkable things about being human is we experience life in two ways. One is external, the other internal.

There is an external reality that exists "out there." That is probably what most people mean when they talk about "reality" or the "real world." It is the world right in front of you and all around you and includes everything you can see, taste, touch, hear, and feel. It is the outside world. It is the chair you are sitting in, the table or desk right in front of you, the lamp, the walls, the floors and ceilings.

Not only is there the external world, there is also an internal representation of the external world in your mind. Your mind contains a model of the outside world, and it is a model of your creation.

For instance, if you stop for a moment and close your eyes, you should be able to get an aerial visualization of the city where you live and where that city is in relation to the other cities or towns nearby. You should be able to conjure, in your mind's eye, a picture of your house and your place of work and where your friends and family live. You should be able get an image in your mind of where you would go to catch the bus and where it might take you. All of these images and visualizations are based on the model of the world you have created in your mind. If it weren't for the model in your mind, how else would you be able to navigate safely through your home during a blackout?

But here's the problem:

The model can mislead us and cause a great deal of stress and misery, especially when it involves people. This is due to the fact that the model includes copies of all the people you perceive in your life and those copies, which are based on your perceptions, cannot perfectly match the originals that exist in the world.

This is to say that when you meet someone, they exist in two places. They exist in reality, and they exist in your mind, and the two are different. In short, your internal model of reality is not the same as external reality.

Let's say you meet someone, and you think he or she is completely awesome. This person is exceptionally engaging, laughs at your jokes, and gives you compliments. But for the sake of argument, let's say this person is really a fraud and none of what you are experiencing is authentic or sincere. Nevertheless, based on your experience and perceptions, the image you create in your mind is that of someone who is sincere and friendly and someone you can trust. However, in actuality, the image you have created in your mind is not the same as "the reality" of the person, so later, when you learn the person is a con artist, your reaction is naturally one of disappointment and shock.

Here is another variation.

How many times have you been talking to a friend or a colleague, and they were speaking favorably about someone you didn't think too much of? Do you remember how you felt? Did you try to sway them over to your way of thinking? In a case like that, more than likely, it is disturbing to discover the image you have in your mind does not match what others perceive. This is disturbing because, by implication, it means your image is flawed and not only that, but by further implication, it means you are potentially defective for having created a flawed image of someone else.

So what are we saying exactly?

We are saying you need people in your life, but you need to be careful how you perceive them. You need to be *mindful* that your perception of others is different from the reality of them.

People are who they are. They are not who we imagine them to be. If we believe the image we have of someone in our mind is the same as that person in reality, we are setting ourselves up for trouble.

People can be wonderful, but do not let yourself fall into the trap of believing the reflection is the person. Do not confuse the sheet music for the song or the book for the movie. They are copies of originals, renditions of renditions, all subject to individual interpretation.

Here's another example.

Let's say you are sitting in a bar, drinking a drink, and listening to a nicely dressed man playing a grand piano. For a few minutes there, you find yourself enjoying the music and decide to give him a tip. You pull out a couple of dollars, stroll over the piano, and smile while you put the money into a prominently displayed vase. You look straight at him, but he does not look at you and keeps right on playing. He doesn't acknowledge you in the slightest.

It seems odd not to get even a head nod, but you don't say anything and walk back to your table. You try to get back into the music, but now you find yourself wondering why the guy didn't even acknowledge you. You let it get the better of you and suddenly, in your mind, the piano player is a bum, a loser, a deadbeat with no social skills, and you even manage to promise yourself that you will never tip another musician again.

The music stops.

You watch "the bum" closely. He appears to be stopping for a break.

You watch closely as he stands, grabs a stick with his right hand from under the piano, and places his left hand on the side of the piano and slowly guides himself to the bathroom. Right then, a sinking feeling goes straight to your gut, and you couldn't feel more ashamed of yourself.

He is blind!

Again, reality and our perceptions are separate things, easily confused as one and the same. Troubles arise when our internal images of reality mislead us and for that reason, we recommend being careful in how you view others. If you are not, then what you are doing will be based on perception, not the actual person and that can be a dangerous thing.

CHAPTER 30
PEOPLE ARE LIKE THE WEATHER, SO BE PREPARED

"I can't change the direction of the wind, but I can adjust my sails to always reach my destination."
Jimmy Dean

Moving right along, we hope you can appreciate how complicated relationships can be. As you can see, while they are central to our happiness, they are also central to our problems. If anything, people are so complicated they often defy forecasting. Yet the way our minds work, we love to predict and forecast. It makes life easier, though not necessarily better.

It is the complicated nature of people that makes us want to forecast them, but the truth is we are doing a disservice to ourselves and others when we do that.

For instance, it could be that someone you don't care for could be the best person to have in your life. And on the other side, it could also be that someone you care for is the worst person for you. But how would you know if you are making preemptive decisions based on your forecasts of them?

When we meet someone who is difficult, it is so much easier to name them like a hurricane and avoid them altogether. And mind you, as we will be discussing in an upcoming section, there are definitely situations that might warrant doing that, but it should be the exception, not the rule.

We can try to say this person is good and that person is bad, but the reality is people are rarely one extreme or the other. Most people fall on a continuum. Most people are probably partly cloudy with a chance of showers, some of this and some of that. Does this mean we completely avoid someone because they could rain on us? What if we are wrong? Who loses in that situation?

We want you to have as many people in your life as is reasonably possible, but we want you to remember people are like the weather. And what we mean by this is you should always be prepared when you are dealing with them. And like the weather, do not rely too much on forecasts. Things change. People can too.

People are indeed central to our well-being, yet we need to be prepared for whatever they might bring. The worst thing you can do is not be prepared and rely on a bad forecast.

CHAPTER 31
THE ALL-POWERFUL SMILE

"There are hundreds of languages in the world, but a smile speaks them all."
Author Unknown

Of all the things we talk about in this book, we would be remiss if we didn't talk about smiling and why we believe it is so important.

There is one theory floating around about how smiles started. The theory claims that smiles evolved from primates who showed their teeth as a way to communicate they meant no harm to a potential adversary. We suppose this was the dental equivalent of putting your hands in the air with your palms facing out. We don't know if we buy that theory completely.

What we do know is that smiling is universally recognized across all cultures as a way of communicating pleasure and happiness. There are exceptions to this, but for the most part, smiling is one of those rare things everyone understands. If you are smiling, we do not have to speak your language to know what is going on with you. And today, with so many misunderstandings in the world, that is something we could use more of. Smiling is a good thing, a universally-recognized thing, a nonverbal form of communication nearly everyone can use and understand. Smiling is also immediate, one-to-one, one-to-many, and can leave a lasting impression. Smiles are welcoming and symbolize the best aspects of our collective humanity.

In naming this book *Pass The Smiles*, we chose that title because it incorporates two major tenets of our philosophy.

First is the belief that happiness mandates action. You are not going to magically become happy thinking about it. You have to make a move and take an action. You'll notice the title is not *Think* The Smiles. It is *Pass* The Smiles. It is an action. You've got to do it!

Second is the deeper belief you have to do something positive for others. We sincerely believe that you can't be truly happy in this life unless you are consistently stepping it up and doing something meaningful for others. We also believe that once you begin to do positive things for others, it will have a cascade effect, and you will begin to notice across-the-board improvements in your life.

Now here is the nice thing. How much do smiles cost? How many calories do smiles burn? How much effort does it take to smile? Nothing, none, and none! That's right. One of the nicest things you can do for someone is absolutely free and takes virtually no effort. What more could you ask for?

If you can bring yourself to smile more, you will have taken a huge step forward on the path to sustained happiness. The act of smiling will trigger a host of incalculable positive effects. Here's a partial rundown:

- You will be taking a positive action and triggering your mind to think more positively.

- You will be making others feel better, more comfortable, and happier.

- You will be setting an example for others.

- You will be reinforcing the themes of this book in your mind and increasing the overall chances for your sustained happiness.

- You will be creating a more positive world for yourself and others.

- And over time, you will become happier.

If you find yourself resistant to smiling more, we would say you need to quit thinking about it and just do it. You might not feel comfortable initially, but you really can pass the smiles!

CHAPTER 32
CREATING A PERSONAL LEGACY

"I expect to pass through life but once. If therefore, there be any kindness I can show, or any good thing I can do to any fellow being, let me do it now, and not defer or neglect it, as I shall not pass this way again."
William Penn

If we were only able to make two or three recommendations to you, one of them would be to work on creating a personal legacy. Creating a legacy holds many of the keys to happiness. It involves giving of yourself, doing something for others, and most important, it requires you to take action. And if you do all those things, lasting fulfillment is likely to follow.

Now we realize you might not have the money to be a philanthropist but that's not what we are suggesting.

By personal legacy, we mean staging your life for how you want to be remembered. Do you want to be remembered as someone who took care of yourself or others? Do you want to be remembered as someone who thought about things or someone who did things? Do you want to be remembered as a happy person? Of course, we realize these are rhetorical questions. Most, if not all of us, want to be remembered as good, kind, and caring individuals. And if you start reaching out and creating good works, then that is how you will be remembered. People will remember what you did and how that made them feel.

Think back on your life. Of all your family and friends, who do you remember and why? More than likely, you remember the ones who looked out for you, did things for you, and cared about you. What they did for you was their legacy, and you remembered! Of course, you might also remember some of the bad things people did, but usually you remember the good things people did for you and how that made you feel.

As we mentioned above, we are not asking you to build a children's hospital or start your own soup kitchen, unless, of course, you can! What we are asking is for you to consider what you can do for others in a way that will outlast your physical existence. It could be the starting of an organization, the writing of a book, or the funding of a scholarship. It could take any possible form and is only limited by your imagination.

We have included, in the appendix, a list of legacy possibilities but really encourage you to come up with your own ideas. Whatever you decide, it should be something you feel passionate about.

Creating a personal legacy is your way of saying you had an idea about why you are here and what life is all about. Creating a legacy will mean you will be remembered after you're gone and that your spiritual energy will live on.

It is sad we don't live forever, but our actions, in the form of a legacy, do.

Think about that for a moment.

Creating a legacy is not only the key to your happiness now—it is a way to immortality. A legacy, in that sense, is the epitome of any action you can take. It is the highest good you can possibly do.

Remember legacies take time and planning. It is never too early to start thinking about what it is you want to do and the earlier you start, the better.

CHAPTER 33
SEE PEOPLE AS PEOPLE AND NOT AS OBJECTS

"When you start treating people like people, they become people."
Paul Vitale

We have been emphasizing people because of the central role they play in our emotional lives. From the moment we are born until the moment we die, we are surrounded and influenced by people. People affect each and every aspect of everything we do.

Even if we wanted to try to forget about everyone and moved as far away as we could, people would still be in our memories during the day and in our dreams at night. In fact, the harder we try to escape from people, the more likely they will exert an influence on us. Other people are an inescapable aspect of our existence. We cannot and do not exist without them.

Yet there is a problem that occurs with the pervasiveness of people in our lives. At some point, we stop seeing people as human beings and start seeing them as objects. Sometimes this happens by necessity and sometimes for convenience, but it happens often and to all of us.

When it does, and we cross that line and start seeing people as objects, we are giving ourselves a license to treat them in any way we want. And when that happens, it is possible for the worst aspects of our personalities to come out. And that is not good for anyone.

Here's an illustration for your consideration.

Let's say you've had a busy day at work and are heading home when you suddenly decide to stop at a drive-through to get a quick bite to eat. You don't think it will take long so you swing by the closest one you can find and pull in. You immediately see there is a long line of cars already backed up, but you pull in anyway. The van in front of you has blacked-out windows, so you can't see who is inside, but you notice they are placing a large order. Ten long minutes pass and except for that van, you are almost to the pickup window. You know they had a big order, so you finally turn off your engine. Time passes excruciatingly slow. The smell of van's exhaust is starting to get to you, so you roll up your window.

You also start wondering what you did in life to deserve this and notice your mind begins an assembly-line production of bad thoughts about the van people and at a certain point, you can't even associate the van with anything remotely human. It is just a thing with things in it. The people aren't people. They are obstacles, irritants, shadows, and empty shells taking up space. And it is at this point that you cross an invisible line and are now wishing the van and every *thing* in it would simply disappear.

Finally, you can see the attendant instructs the van's driver to pull up and park to the side. There must have been a problem with their order. You give a sigh of relief, drive up, and get your order.

You are still simmering in your stew of bad thoughts and as you are getting ready to drive away, you can't help but glance over at the vile van people who took fifteen minutes from your life. You turn and see it is a group of elderly nuns. The nun in the driver's seat shoots you a big toothy smile. You fumble for a matching response and feel about as embarrassed as you possibly could.

What just happened? How did you go from hot to cold so fast? How could you start thinking such bad thoughts about people you couldn't even see or know? Why did you feel ashamed at the end?

In our view, we often can and do see other people as things. It can happen in a drive-through. It can happen in traffic. It can happen in a war. It can happen at anytime to anybody. It seems the only way we can truly treat each other badly is when we see each other as things, not as human beings.

The fact of the matter is we are at our worst when we see people as objects and seeing people that way is the polar opposite of passing the smiles. When people are things, they are not people any longer. Turning people into objects is how we justify doing things we would not do to ourselves and that will not lead us to happiness. When we see people as objects, we take away their humanity and ironically, a little of our own at the same time.

The best way not to turn people into objects is by being aware you are doing it in the first place. Awareness leads to control. When you see people as people, you see them as you see yourself and that's what is needed to pass the smiles.

CHAPTER 34
ASSOCIATE WITH AS MANY POSITIVE PEOPLE AS POSSIBLE

"Really great people make you feel that you, too, can become great."
Mark Twain

Isn't it interesting that we experience people through every sense we have? We hear them. We see them. We smell them. We feel them. You could even say there are no boundaries among us. We breathe the same air, live in the same places, and share the same experiences. People are you, and you are people, and we permeate each other.

People affect the totality of our being. Think about the last time someone made you laugh hard. Think about the last time someone made you cry. Didn't it affect your whole sense of everything? Didn't it resonate through your entire being and color everything around you?

Look at the expressions we use.

If someone can "rub you the wrong way," then someone else can most certainly "rub off" on you. In our estimation, people profoundly influence us and that's why we need to be careful who we let into our personal lives.

When we say you should associate with as many positive people as possible, we are not asking you to pass judgment on anyone. We are asking you to keep in mind the definitions of positive and negative and to trust your feelings. For instance, if someone makes you feel good or makes you laugh most of the time when you are together, *and* this person is having no adverse effects on you, then we would say this is someone you need to keep in your life. This is someone you should consider seeing more often or doing more things with.

On the other hand, if someone makes you feel bad most of the time when you are together, then this is someone you shouldn't be spending too much time with.

The theory is simple.

You are fighting a battle against yourself and the world to stay positive. You don't need any more negativity in your life than you have already. You need positive energy, positive thinking, and positive action. You need to surround yourself with people who make you feel alive.

It shouldn't take much effort to identify those people in your life who make you feel happy. From there, all you need to do is make an effort to spend more time with them and make them feel as good as they are making you feel.

CHAPTER 35
STOP ASSOCIATING WITH NEGATIVE PEOPLE OR MINIMIZE YOUR TIME WITH THEM

"You have the right to quit Toxic People. (They're contagious.)"
Dr. Sun

We hate the idea of labeling people but sometimes we have to. To our way of thinking, labeling someone as bad influence is a last resort. You should take the matter of labeling someone as negative with a great sense of responsibility. Think of it as major law being passed. It should be studied and analyzed and thought through before it is done because it can have far-reaching consequences. We don't want you to get into the habit of passing judgment on others, but you have to do what is right for you and your goals, especially if your ultimate aim is for the greater good.

In a previous section, we talked about people being like the weather. We tried to make the case that just because someone is having a bad day every now and then is no reason to avoid them completely. However, when it comes to truly toxic people, it is more like the climate of an area versus the day-to-day weather. For instance, you don't need a weather report in Antarctica. It is always cold. And so it is with a minority of people—some people are bad for you, and you have to take action to lessen their effect on you.

Probably the biggest question is how do you know if someone is truly a toxic influence in your life? There is no easy answer for that. However, we would say to trust your feelings. Your emotional reactions to people are not necessarily factual or accurate, but they are your feelings, and you are having them for a reason. Plus, we firmly believe you have an absolute right to your feelings, and they serve a vital purpose.

We have heard some say that we have outgrown the need for our emotions in modern society and that our emotions do nothing but cause trouble. We believe the opposite is true. We believe many problems are due to discounting and denying emotions. We believe society is placing too much emphasis on thinking and not enough on feeling. We believe emotions are the solution, not the problem!

So, with regard to the question of how will you know who is negative, the answer is to go by how that person makes you feel. For instance, if after every time you talk to someone, you end up feeling bad about yourself, then that's probably something to seriously consider as an indicator. If someone makes jokes at your expense, belittles you in front of others, or screams at you for no reason, then these are all signs you are not in a healthy relationship.

Now we most certainly realize you do not always get to choose who will be in your life. You do not usually have a choice of coworkers and family. You are often forced to interact with certain people, even on a daily basis. So if you are in a situation where you are forced to interact with someone who is toxic to you, then our advice is to minimize your time with them and keep things on a business-like level.

What this means is if you are forced into a situation with a toxic person, don't offer any more of yourself than you absolutely have to. Be polite but keep things focused on the tasks at hand and nothing more. Do not share personal stories or make yourself vulnerable to this person in any way.

To summarize:

There are three kinds of people in this world—those who are good for you, those who are bad, and those who are somewhere in-between. Most people fall in the middle and like the weather, you have to be prepared for them every day. For the ones who are bad for you, you need to get them out of your life and if you can't, then keep all of your interactions with them to an absolute minimum. For those who are good for you, you need to make a special effort to spend more time with them and do more things with them.

CHAPTER 36
MAKE ONE PERSON SMILE EACH DAY

"A smile happens in a flash, but its memory can last a lifetime."
Author Unknown

Smiles are something to wonder about.

How could something so easy to do be so hard to do? How could something so powerful be so easily overlooked in our day-to-day dealings with each other? How could something so fleeting leave an impression that would last a lifetime? How could a smile be so much more meaningful than anything words could say?

Smiles were around before words and even after words escape us, smiles will still be around. Whatever you think about smiles, we don't want you to deny or discount the power they have. We realize a lot of people might smile at you, but there are, no doubt, many more who don't. Many people do not risk a smile, and we want to change that. We want more people smiling and believe this simple gesture can go a long way toward bringing all of us closer.

But where does it start? Do we start wearing buttons with smiles on them? Do we print a billion copies of this book and distribute them across the world? Do we buy television and radio ads?

No. We aren't doing any of that. The answer is this campaign is deeply personal because it starts with you! It is you who is going to make a difference.

And it starts low and slow. All we are asking you to do is to commit to making one person smile each day. How hard is that?

You can start each day with a positive action and that action can be to smile at the first person you see. In fact, the very thought of smiling at someone each day will help to put your mind in a happier state. And we are absolutely convinced if you make this commitment, it will get to a point where it becomes automatic and at that point, you will be on your way toward sustainable happiness.

So dig deep and pass the smiles! Make one person smile each day. Chances are the simple act of smiling will make someone else smile right back at you. If a toddler can muster up a smile, so can you!

CHAPTER 37
LISTEN MORE

"You cannot truly listen to anyone and do anything else at the same time."
M. Scott Peck

Do you think there is a reason we have two ears and only one mouth? Some people think it means we should listen two times more than we talk. We don't know if that's totally true or not, but we do believe we need to spend more time listening to others.

We have been talking about the importance of people in our lives and how much of an influence they have on us. And if you can believe that, then doesn't it make sense we should spend a little more time listening and less time talking? Certainly, when we are talking we are not listening and many times when we appear to be listening, we aren't listening but thinking about what we are going to say next.

One thing about listening is it requires concentration and effort. Maybe that's why we don't do it as much as we should. When someone is talking to you, it is easy to become distracted and not pay attention to what is being said. In addition, when someone is talking, he or she is usually communicating on many levels. And sometimes it can be difficult to decipher what is truly being said. Many times people don't mean what they say or don't say what they mean. Many times people mean the opposite of what they are saying. Many times people are saying something to manipulate a situation or fishing for a particular response. And many times, out of courtesy, people are again giving the appearance of listening when they are not. But what happens when somebody truly listens to you? What does that do?

Let's look at a hypothetical example.

Imagine you work at a sandwich shop and are getting paid minimum wage. They only pay you for five hours of work a day, but it takes seven to get everything done. You feel like you are being taken advantage of and should be making more money for all that you do. You decide it is time to talk to the boss about a raise.

One night, during the closing shift, your boss shows up unexpectedly, says he has some paperwork to catch up on, and heads to his office. After he has settled in and been there for a while, you stop by and ask if he has a moment to speak with you. He looks busy but immediately stops what he is doing and says he does. He invites you in, and you sit in a chair directly across from him. He closes the door, turns off his cell phone, and in a relaxed manner, turns to you and says, "What would you like to talk about?" He is smiling and looking straight at you, giving you his full and undivided attention.

You talk about how much you like your job but then say you were wondering about when you might get a raise. He says he appreciates your work and values you as an employee, then he goes over his formula for raises. He says that after six months, you get a 2% raise, then after a year, 3% more. In a slow and deliberate way, he then asks you how things are going in your life and if there are any other concerns or issues. And as you respond to these questions, you notice he is continuing to listen to you as if you were the most important person in the world. He is leaning forward and intently hanging on your every word. He is nodding as if he understands exactly what you are saying and is right there with you. He makes you feel like a complete and equal partner.

After a while, you have almost forgotten why you even came to his office. And after you leave, even though the raise he has promised is far below what you wanted, you just feel good about him and the company.

And that's how it should be!

When we show others respect by blocking all distractions, giving them our undivided attention, and showing an interest in what they are saying, it means the world to them. In many ways, listening is the ultimate sign of respect. Think about people who disrespect each other. Do they listen to each other? Do they really care what the other has to say?

Listening is respecting and valuing others. It is the key to friendship and lifelong relationships. It is the glue that holds us together.

CHAPTER 38
STOP SNAPPING

"He who angers you conquers you."
Elizabeth Kenny

Getting angry and yelling at someone is the opposite of passing the smiles and that is why we are suggesting you don't do it. In a previous section, we talked about negative emotions serving as warning signs but at the point you are actually yelling or screaming or snapping at someone, you have gone too far and need to pull back. If you find yourself snapping or screaming at someone, then you have lost control.

Now we recognize we have our limits, and it seems inevitable we are going to all snap at some point and that is no doubt true. But we want to make sure that if it happens, it occurs rarely or better yet, not at all. Why do we say that?

Think about how you feel when someone screams at you. Does it bother you? Does it make you feel good? Does it serve any useful purpose at all? Is it productive in any way?

Now we are sure you can conjure the image of a drill sergeant barking at recruits in basic training but that's not what we are talking about. We are talking about your day-to-day world, not boot camp.

So what can you do? How can you keep yourself from getting so angry that you start snapping and screaming?

There is no one-size-fits-all answer, but there are strategies you can try. You can mix and match and find the combination that works best for you. Here are some tips in no particular order.

QUICK TIPS FOR MANAGING ANGER AND FRUSTRATION

- If you feel like you are close to losing it, it is absolutely okay to call a time out and walk away. Don't let anyone tell you differently. How do you know it is time to walk away? Rate your anger on a scale from one to ten, if it is a six or higher, it is time to leave. How long should you be gone? At least ten minutes. Should you say anything before you leave? Possibly. You can say what you have to say without cursing or giving ultimatums but make it quick.

- Keep these thoughts in mind.

    1) The feet you step on today might be connected to the rear end you have to kiss tomorrow.

    2) No situation is worth your emotional health.

    3) To get respect you have to show respect. (And are you showing respect?)

    4) Battles should be weighed, not counted.

    5) The world owes you the same as what you've given it. (And honestly, how much is that?)

    6) You want to live to fight another day.

    7) Yelling in anger means you are operating on raw emotion, not logic. (And is that how you want to make decisions?)

    8) You can undo your thinking but not your actions. Be careful.

- Give yourself one night to sleep on it. See how you feel in the morning. If you still feel angry, then develop a concrete plan to reasonably deal with the situation.

Of course, there are many more strategies than these. We have just chosen a few of our favorites.

Getting and staying angry is the easy way out. Anyone can snap but not just anyone can take the high road and pass the smiles, especially in a situation that might be totally unfair.

You deserve to be treated with respect and so do those around you. We have more in common with each other than we have differences. You can be irritated and agitated and angry. No one is saying you can't. What we are saying is not to take it out on others. Neither you nor anyone else appreciates being the recipient of rage. Take the high road and pass the smiles!

LANGUAGE

CHAPTER 39
BE AWARE OF THE POWER OF LANGUAGE TO STRUCTURE YOUR REALITY

"Language forces us to perceive the world as man presents it to us."
Julia Penelope

Communication takes place on many levels and in many ways. We don't dispute that nonverbal communication is important and that how something is said is often more revealing than what is said. For instance, if someone says, "I am sorry," in an irritated voice, the irritability conveys more meaning than the words. And despite the clear power of the nonverbal, we should never underestimate the power of words by themselves.

When a word is in your mind, it exerts a structural effect on how you perceive reality. Words are the homes where thoughts live, and our minds are vast residential communities. When we start applying words to things or concepts, the thing or concept becomes fixed in our minds and constrained by its own definition. Putting a word on something also makes it seem real when it might only be a figment of someone's imagination or worse, not even true at all.

Let's take some examples.

When you say you "can't" do something, what, in fact, are you saying? Of course, you are saying you cannot do something but does that mean you really can't do it? It is hard to say, but more than likely when you say you can't do something, you are really saying you don't want to do it. There's a big difference.

Try this experiment to see for yourself. Stop saying "I can't" and replace it with "I don't want to." See what kind of an effect that has. You might be surprised at how much control you really have.

Putting words on things freezes them in your mind's eye. Words solidify the things they represent and give them credence, even if they have no credence at all.

When Sigmund Freud developed his theory of psychology, he had a concept and came up with a name for it. He called it the "ego." Now did Freud discover the ego in a laboratory or did he make it up? If we remember correctly, he made it up. But do you see what happened once he gave his idea a name? The word brought the idea into existence, fixed it in our minds, and made it a "reality."

Here's another example.

It has been said people who live in the arctic region have more than ten words for snow. Why is that? The obvious answer is since they live in the snow, they have observed variations in snow worth noting for their purposes. In this case, reality is the inspiration for the words and the words, in turn, help bring reality into a sharper and possibly more useful focus. But let us ask this: If someone has ten words for snow, does that really mean there are ten types of snow? Do the words, even though they are inspired from reality, change the nature of reality?

Words change your perception of reality, but the true nature of reality cannot be known by you. You will perceive reality based on your experiences and interpretations. And a significant part of how you perceive things will, in fact, be based on language. Language is our tool for conveniently managing our perceptions. That's why we want you to be aware of the words you use and how they might be tainting your perceptions.

For instance, when you call somebody a bad name, you are contaminating your mind. How?

Because you have frozen that person in your world, and now they can only be what you've called them. In other words, words have the power to condemn people and lock in our perceptions of them forever and that is in no way a good thing.

For example, let's say somebody at work goes to your supervisor over something that was an honest mistake on your part, and you get a written reprimand. If the person had kept quiet, nothing would have happened. But they didn't, so now you've got this write-up in your personnel file at work. You are pretty upset about the incident and after it is all over, you start referring to this person as a "stinking rat." And as you say that to yourself and your friends, you start noticing that this person kind of looks like a rat and not much longer after that, you can't even stand to look at "the rat."

Can you see the problem?

Even though you might have every reason in the world to be angry with this person, using harsh language is not the answer. Words, especially pejorative ones, are like toxic cement. By casting any person in such terms, not only will that person become more poisonous to you in reality, that person will also exist in your mind and take up space! Do you really need that? A stinking rat in your mind?

Think of language as something that has the power to change things from what they are. Think of language as something that should be carefully dispensed and weighed. Talk may be cheap, but words can be expensive if we are not cautious.

CHAPTER 40
FEEL THE FEELING

"Our feelings are our most genuine paths to knowledge."
Audre Lorde

In the prior section, we were talking about the power of language to structure reality and influence perceptions. Now here is more bad news: Words are also inadequate in helping us to understand each other and reality. Meaning and truth do exist, but words have a hard time capturing them.

Need a quick example?

Imagine someone you know has recently passed away. Everyone you know who knew this person is upset. A group of you decide to send flowers and a card to the surviving family. The card is circulating and when it gets to you, you are the last one to sign it. As such, you also get to read what everyone else has written and see all the usual expressions such as: "You are in our thoughts and prayers," "We are thinking about you," and "With deepest sympathy." But as nice as those sentiments are, you just can't seem to find the words to express the loss you are feeling. In fact, you can't even think of anything to say, even though this is someone you knew well.

Why is it so hard to come up with something to say?

In our opinion, it is hard to come up with something to say because words don't always work well when describing feelings and reality. You can't put emotions in a box, label them, and stack them on library shelves. Words work for many things, but for relationships, they fail miserably.

At one point, we were trying to explain the feeling we get when we help somebody who needs and appreciates it. And that is when it occurred to us that there are no words that can sufficiently describe that feeling. There are no words that do it justice. But whatever that feeling is, we know it when we feel it, and we know it's a good thing.

Our point is you need to get out and do good things for others and when you do, you will get "this feeling" about what you did. We won't describe what the feeling is. You need to feel the feeling for yourself and when you do, it should feel good enough that you'll want to keep getting that same feeling over and over.

Words are powerful and saying the right things at the right time can profoundly influence others. But words cannot fully capture the essence of what it feels like to be truly happy inside. Words can never capture how you felt on the happiest day of your life. No doubt you can try to capture what things feel like with words, but words cannot replace the experience.

When you do the positive things we recommend in this book, stay aware of your feelings.

CHAPTER 41
DO NOT USE WORDS THAT CLAIM OWNERSHIP

"No man can lose what he never had."
Izaak Walton

If you are still having some doubts about the power of words to structure your reality and influence your perceptions, we would like to challenge you to a little experiment.

The challenge is simple and only requires you to stop saying two words for three days. The two words are "my" and "mine." Do you think you can do it? Do you think dropping these words from your vocabulary will have any effect on you? The only way you'll know is to try it and see what happens.

Before you begin the experiment it might be helpful to know why we chose these two words and explain our thinking.

To start, the words "my" and "mine" denote ownership and possession. And at first glance, ownership and possession seem perfectly harmless. But in keeping with our experience, possession and ownership are contrived constructs that bring out the worst in us.

For a moment, think about a 3-year-old boy who is playing with another child in his room. The boy "owns" a small mountain of toys already and has plenty to share but when the other child starts playing with one, the boy grabs it and yells, "Mine!"

What thoughts come into your mind about the boy? Are they positive or negative? Do you think the boy grasps the true meaning of possession? If you were his parent, what would be your reaction? How would his behavior make you feel?

Now let's imagine a little different example.

Let's say you live in an apartment complex and have been on friendly terms with your next-door neighbor for a couple of years. Your complex has a common laundry area with washers and dryers. One day you take a load of clothes to the laundry and notice all the washing machines are in use. You come back thirty minutes later and notice the machines have stopped running but whoever put the clothes in the washing machines hasn't come to get them out. A big sign on the wall clearly reads: *Do not leave your clothes unattended*. You need to wash your clothes, so you carefully take the clothes out of one machine, place them on a table, then put your clothes in and start the washer. Ten minutes later, your neighbor enters the laundry and looks over at the clothes on the table. Your neighbor shoots you a dirty look and puts the clothes in the dryer. You say, "I hope you don't mind I took your clothes out, but I really needed to get the laundry done." Your neighbor says, "I'd appreciate it if you wouldn't mess with *my* clothes in *my* machine again."

How would that honestly make you feel? Would you be angry or understanding? Do you believe your neighbor has a right to claim ownership of the washer?

We believe the degree to which you are attached to material possessions is the same degree to which you will experience pain at their ultimate loss. Wouldn't it be better to view any items you "own" as things you are just lucky to be able to have under your temporary control and that they could be gone tomorrow? Do material possessions make us truly happy? Is the person who has the most things really the winner?

The truth is we came into this world with nothing and will leave with nothing. The words "my" and "mine" might have meaning in this life but not in any possible afterlife. Your pure human spirit has no need for material possessions now or in the future. The sooner we disconnect from material things, the better.

And yet, while you can still disregard this and claim ownership of *things*, you can never "own" another person. Even if you think you can, you can't. To believe you possess another is to believe you can own a distant star. It is a grand illusion.

We believe claiming ownership and possession is a precursor to loss and creates an illusion you have "a right" to something you don't or are only using for a relatively short time. Contrary to social expectations, you are better off with less.

If you don't agree this is true, then try not using the words "my" and "mine" for three days. See how it makes you feel. You might feel a strange resistance. No doubt it will feel awkward. But you might also notice it has a distancing and calming effect too. Either way, you have nothing to lose except a sense of attachment to things that are only weighing you down.

CHAPTER 42
LIMIT THE USE OF ABSOLUTE WORDS

"Be not the slave of words."
Thomas Carlyle

We find ourselves in a paradox here because we are close to saying, "Never say never." It only makes us a feel a little better to also say, "Never say always." Those two words, *never* and *always,* can frequently cause problems and trip you up on the road to greater happiness.

Why?

Because those two words lead to extreme thinking and that is rarely a good thing. Most of the time, when you use absolute words, your conclusions are faulty and not completely true. In short, absolute thinking leads to errors in thinking and problems in communication.

Think about it for a moment.

How often do you say *never* and *always*? And if you are honest with yourself, is what you are saying true when you use those words?

Imagine you are in an argument with someone close to you, and you say something like, "You never help out. Never!" And let's say you are basically correct, and this person has only helped you once in the last year. Even though you are "basically correct," you're still wrong. And of course, because you are incorrect, the person you are upset with will undoubtedly come back with, "That's not true. I helped out last year." And now your credibility is at issue when that wasn't even the initial issue. You rarely win when you are thinking in extreme terms because your actions are not based on the complete truth of the situation, and the truth requires totality.

Things can *never* and *always* happen. For instance, the sun, at least for our life spans, will always rise and set. But the sun will not *always* rise. It is scheduled to burn out in four to five billion years and so at some point, it will not even be around to rise and set.

But when it comes to people, exceptions are more the rule. It is usually a good policy to avoid words that are completely exclusive, inclusive, absolute, or extreme.

There are many words that convey a sense of taking things to an extreme. *Always* and *never* are probably the two biggest culprits, but there are other words and expressions that carry the same meaning. For example, *constantly*, *all the time*, and *forever* have the same effect.

A general rule of thumb is to think about what you are saying and imagine it as either a question on a college exam or front-page headline in a newspaper and then ask yourself if what are you saying would hold up to mass scrutiny. In short, is what you are saying true *every* single time? If not, then it is usually better to say nothing than to say something that is false. And when it comes to dealing with others, there are few things worse than saying something that's not true.

CHAPTER 43
DO NOT USE NEGATIVE OR MEAN-SPIRITED LANGUAGE

"Better to light a candle than to curse the darkness."
Chinese Proverb

At the beginning of this section on language, we talked a little about why it is not good to say bad things about others. We want to go over that a bit more because we believe making this change in your life will be one of the most positive things you can do.

Looking into this more, isn't it fascinating how fast bad thoughts can pop into your mind? Do you ever wonder where all that negativity is coming from and how it can come into your mind so quickly?

Of course, we believe it happens so fast because the negativity is already in you. We believe you absorb negativity from the world, and then it literally becomes a part of you.

We also believe this is true from our observations of children who can't say a bad word if they have never seen or heard it. And once they have and repeat it, then depending on the reaction they receive from those around them, they will either keep saying it or not. But either way, the word remains inside them, most likely for a long time. This is why many parents try to control what their children are exposed to.

Let's talk more about why you shouldn't say bad and mean-spirited things in general.

Assume someone is treating you unfairly, is talking behind your back, and is saying all kinds of nasty things about you. Once you learn of this, you, by most measures, are naturally upset and automatically start thinking bad thoughts about this person. You might even come up with some fairly vicious names for this individual and start sharing some of the worst names with your closest associates. But when you do this, when you conjure up vicious names for someone, who does it hurt? Does it hurt you or the other person more?

In our opinion, it hurts you more.

Let us explain.

When you create a word or name for somebody and breathe life into it by saying it, you bring that word and what it represents into a high-definition existence in your mind. The labeling of someone causes that person to become the label. If you label someone as "a jerk," then they become a jerk, not only in the real world but *in your mind*.

The worst thing about this process is once someone becomes that label in your mind, then it is hard to change and get out of your mind. So, in essence, when you call somebody a bad name, you are not only condemning that person to be perceived in reality that way, you are also giving that person permanent residence in your mind as a negative object. In short, when you give somebody a bad name, you are condemning yourself and that person at the same time.

And here's the thing: You have every right to your feelings and perceptions. No one is disputing that or trying to take that away from you. If someone has upset or hurt you, you have a license to think and feel any way you want. But when you cross that invisible line and start calling someone names, you are twice the victim—once at the hand of that person and once at yours. And the hand you deal yourself is worse than the hand you have been dealt because now that person will take up permanent residence in your mind as yet another toxic element.

Why do that to yourself?

Take the higher ground. Be the bigger person and pass the smiles. Don't fall to the temptation of name-calling or disparaging others. It is a no-win situation for you in the end and will not take you where you want to go.

THOUGHTS

CHAPTER 44
THOUGHTS ARE IMPORTANT BUT HARD TO CHANGE AND ISOLATE

"The mind commands the body and it obeys. The mind orders itself and meets resistance."
Saint Augustine

Although you wouldn't know this from watching television, we live in an intellectual world. And by intellectual, we mean a world that places a premium on thinking and holds great thinkers in high regard. After all, who doesn't look up to a thinker?

For instance, if someone says you are "thoughtful" or "intelligent," isn't that one of the nicest compliments you can be paid? On the other hand, if someone says you are "stupid" or "ignorant," then isn't that one of the worst?

Imagine this.

Astronomers discover a huge asteroid is heading for the earth and will destroy all of humankind as we know it. The only hope for humanity's survival is on the international space station, but unfortunately, it can only hold 100 people. Who would be the people chosen and why? Wouldn't our choices reflect what we value about ourselves? In our estimation, more than a few "great thinkers" would make the cut.

We could probably write another book about *why* we place so much value on thinking and thought, but for now, we want to make the point that modern society places thinking above all else, including feeling and acting. You might even say we live in a "thinkist" society where thoughts are worshipped, and thinking is the key to solving all problems, and everything else is secondary.

What are the implications of living in a world that places thinking and thought above all else?

Probably one of the biggest and most obvious implications is every problem is seen as requiring thought to solve. And for many real-world problems, no doubt, the solution can be found in thinking carefully about it. However, when people are involved, this approach begins to falter. Trying to solve a person's problem by "thinking" alone is a nearly impossible task. We can never be sure what is going on in someone's mind and even if we could, the solution wouldn't automatically come by way of thought.

For example, let's say you are in good health, have a great job, and a nice family but, for some unknown reason, you don't feel happy. You don't use drugs or drink alcohol. Nothing *bad* has happened; you just, for some reason, don't feel happy about your life.

Further let's say one day you decide to get away from it all and drive to the beach. You hike to a quiet spot to relax and enjoy nature.

It turns out to be an unbelievable day. You are just sitting there and trying to enjoy the sky, the ocean, and the sound of the waves. You see sailboats in the distance and fishermen near the shore. You could not ask for a more lovely and picturesque day. But as you are sitting there and trying to enjoy some of the best of what the world has to offer, you still don't feel happy. You feel negative and in that state of mind, you are managing to project it to the world around you. And at that very moment, you realize the negativity you are feeling is not *in* the world but *in you*. It is almost as if your thoughts are a dirty window through which an otherwise beautiful view is ruined.

And what's more you cannot, for the life of you, escape your viewpoint. Your thoughts hound you, yet they are also elusive and virtually impossible to control. And so you sit there, not enjoying what should be the perfect day but simmering in your stew of negativity.

What else can *you do*?

We believe the answer is found in the question itself. *You do*! You don't think or try to pinpoint which thoughts are bothering you. You make a course for yourself in life that is one you believe in and one that involves being with and helping others, and once your course is charted, you set sail, you go, you do! You stop thinking about things and start making things happen. And if you do this, those thoughts that ruined your day at the beach will fade in time.

CHAPTER 45
START EACH DAY WITH A POSITIVE THOUGHT

"Be pleasant until ten o'clock in the morning and the rest of the day will take care of itself."
Elbert Hubbard

This is one of those recommendations that is easy for us to make but hard to get in the habit of doing. This one, however, should be easier to do if you followed the suggestion from the chapter on fostering a positive environment and have started putting inspirational sayings and pictures around your living and working spaces.

We find it curious that it is such a challenge to start each day on a positive note. It really shouldn't be that hard but for some reason, especially on some mornings, it can seem like a Herculean task. We believe we know one reason why and that's due to what we have made central to our lives.

Often what we spend the most time doing becomes the centerpiece of our lives and many times, it should not be. For instance, you can say there are two kinds of people in the world—those who live to work and those who work to live. In our experience, those who don't like their job (we're sure there are a few of those around!) *and* who live for their jobs are putting themselves in a bad position because they are building their lives around something they don't even care about. What a recipe for disaster that is! And then there are those who still don't like their job or what they do, but they don't see it as the center of their lives—they only see work as a means to an end, so they can live and pursue what is important to them. These people are much happier.

If you are finding it difficult to start each day on a positive note, then try returning to the three goals we asked you earlier to create.

Those goals should be about what is important to you in your life and what will move you toward greater happiness. Those goals should also be things you feel passionate about and can be accomplished in a short time (six months or less). Those goals can be the center of your life and focus. Those goals will be the line to pull you out of whatever hole you might have fallen in.

If you are still finding it a challenge to be inspired the first thing in the morning , you might also try placing an inspirational item near where you wake up—that way you'll be sure to see it first thing when you open your eyes.

We realize it takes determination to stay positive and to start each day on an upbeat note, but it is worth the effort and will pay off in time. If the sun can rise every day, then you can find something positive in the new day too. Come on! We know you can pass the smiles. You just have to try.

CHAPTER 46
SEE THESE CONCEPTS IN THINGS YOU SEE EVERY DAY

"The metaphor is perhaps one of man's most fruitful potentialities. Its efficacy verges on magic, and it seems a tool for creation which God forgot inside one of His creatures when He made him."
Jose Ortega y Gasset

We keep saying each one of these sections is important because each one is. All of these sections and suggestions are like bricks in a wall; each one serves a purpose and if any one of them were missing, the wall would not be as strong. The suggestion that follows is one of the key concepts in the whole book and something we believe will be absolutely necessary to your long-term happiness.

We have been repeating the idea you are battling two forces at once in trying to be happy—the negative parts of the world *and* the negative parts of yourself. And with those two forces against you, you need all the help you can get. But how do you take on the world? Isn't that a little much?

Let's talk about that for a moment.

When dealing with the world, you are up against something that is coming at you 24-7 and is pretty much everywhere. Not all of it is negative, but many things aren't exactly positive either. We want to level the playing field, so we want you to start seeing the concepts in this book in things you see every day. We want you to create a situation where you redefine the world in a way that benefits you and your efforts toward happiness.

We have a list of nine things and want you to start to see and define these things in a new way. Some of this won't come naturally to you, but with practice, you can turn the world into a more positive place and give yourself a winning chance against it all.

REAL-WORLD IMAGE	WHEN YOU SEE THE IMAGE, DEFINE IT AS THIS:
RED TRAFFIC LIGHT	STOP ALL NEGATIVE THINKING
GREEN TRAFFIC LIGHT	GET GOING ON YOUR GOALS
STOP SIGN	STOP SNAPPING AT OTHERS
A GARDEN OR PARK	TAKE TIME TO RELAX
ANYTHING UNDER CONSTRUCTION	BUILDING YOUR PERSONAL LEGACY
BILLBOARDS	JOURNAL THE POSITIVE
SUN	EXPERIENCE ONE INSPIRATIONAL THING DAILY
FENCES OR WALLS	DO NOT USE WORDS THAT CLAIM OWNERSHIP
CLOUDS	PEOPLE ARE LIKE THE WEATHER, BE PREPARED

You do not have to stick with these nine items and can add those of your own choosing and creation. In fact, it would be better if you did. These are only starting points. We hope you can see how using this method puts you in control and uses the world in a positive way!

CHAPTER 47
STOP THINKING NEGATIVELY

"You must not allow yourself to dwell for a single moment on any kind of negative thought."
Emmet Fox

It seems to us that not only are we bombarded with negativity from the world, but we bombard ourselves with our own negativity. Whether the negativity we have comes entirely from the outside world or is our own creation, we seem to have an unlimited internal supply. And it is all available at a moment's notice!

So here is a hypothetical situation for you.

Let's say you have been following all the recommendations we have made in this book and are trying to reach out to others and pass the smiles. You happen to step in an elevator and see a woman who glances at you for a second, then looks away. You are making a conscious effort to be positive and pass the smiles, so you smile and say, "Good morning." She doesn't acknowledge you in any way and keeps staring straight ahead. You try to think of excuses for her but the more you think about it, the angrier it makes you. And before you know it your attempt at "passing the smiles" has blown up right in your face because now instead of being happy, you are upset and thinking all kinds of bad things about this woman.

What happened? How did a tiny gesture of goodwill trigger such an avalanche of negativity?

In our opinion, our negative selves are more developed than our positive ones, much like a weight lifter who exercises one body part over all the others. The result is like a strong-arm punch, forceful and immediate. How else can you explain the sheer number of the negative thoughts you can conjure up, not to mention the speed at which they attack?

Now we are not saying we think there is anything wrong with you, or you are a terrible monster walking the streets. We are not saying that at all. The negativity that is in you is the same kind in all of us. But knowing this, knowing there is this reservoir of negativity inside each and every one of us, what are we to do? How are we to manage it?

The first step, of course, is to be aware you are being negative. The second is to stop it before it gets out of hand.

How do you stop it?

The same way you stop anyone from doing something that bothers you. You say or yell, "STOP IT." That's right. The technique is called thought-stopping.

It works like this:

When you find yourself becoming agitated or being overtaken by your negative thoughts, visualize a STOP sign and tell yourself to "*stop it.*" Some people recommend putting a rubber band around your wrist and snapping it each time you have a negative thought, but we think it works better to tell yourself, out loud, to stop it. We find one of the best places to do this is in a car because you can yell without bothering anyone or drawing undue attention.

Now we realize this suggestion might sound too simple to be true, but it does help. You have to make it a habit though and start consistently telling yourself to stop thinking negatively as soon as you become aware of it.

We tell other people to stop what they are doing nearly every day and for the most part, it works. It also works on yourself, but it takes time and awareness to get good at doing it. So go ahead and *stop it!*

CHAPTER 48
REDEFINE YOUR PAST

"The past is a work in progress."
Greg Keast

In many ways, the past is the best predictor of the future. To know where someone is going you only have to look at where they've been; however, this isn't always the case.

Think about someone who committed a crime as a young adult. Does the fact that someone committed a crime once mean he or she will commit a crime again? Should someone's entire future be condemned because of one mistake from the past?

These are tough questions we don't have easy answers for. But we have to admit the past does play a major role in shaping our futures. However, when it comes right down to it, we do not believe one's future is locked in place because of what has happened in the past.

Let us explain.

Many think of the past as something that is done and over and set in concrete. We look back at things we have done and possibly regret and say to ourselves, "What's done is done. I can't change the past." And that is absolutely true. However, do you have to remember all the bad things from your past? Do you have to bring *all* the past forward with you?

Our answer is absolutely not!

It is true you can't change the past, but it is also true you can choose what to focus on from your past and in that sense, define the past in a way that helps your future.

For instance, look at what nations do. Nations are selective about what they choose to commemorate from the past. They might celebrate the day they became independent or won a war or joined a league of nations. What they bring forward from the past all depends on what they desire for their future. If something from the past is beneficial for them to remember, then they remember it. If it is not, then they forget it.

It is intriguing if you think about it.

Nations have a definite agenda to keep the nation-state strong and proud and unified and what they bring from the past, even if it is a day of sorrow or victimization, is all geared in that direction.

If entire nations can do this on a grand scale, why can't you do it? Why wouldn't you?

We are not saying you should turn your back on your past. We are saying exactly the opposite—take a good look at your past but only commemorate those things that are going to move your life in a positive direction. Everything else is better left where it is—in the past.

CHAPTER 49
ALIGN YOURSELF WITH YOURSELF

"Identity would seem to be the garment with which one covers the nakedness of the self, in which case, it is best that the garment be loose, a little like the robes of the desert, through which one's nakedness can always be felt, and, sometimes, discerned."
James Arthur Baldwin

Without a doubt, humans are complicated. There is no way around that fact. We have a complex brain that produces an even more sophisticated mind and spirit. We have access to billions of bits of information that are all interlinked and intertwined beyond comprehension. Our brains exist as a neural network that cannot be read, predicted, or fully understood. And for the thousands of years that we have been around as civilized beings, we still don't understand ourselves and haven't figured out how to stop killing each other.

In short, we are almost too complicated for our own good. We exist as walking contradictions encompassing everything that is good and bad, right and wrong, and true and false. And the harder someone tries to pin us down, the more we resist and defy them if for no other reason than to resist and defy them. We think we know ourselves, but most of the time we don't have a clue about what we are doing or why. And if someone told us that they had it all figured out, we wouldn't believe them.

We have been talking about how you view the world and others, but now we want to spend some time talking about how you view yourself. Unfortunately, that's no simple subject to tackle in a section this small, so we will only be touching on a few basic concepts.

To start, we believe there are at least four competing versions of you. These are:

1. How you see yourself (your private self)

2. How you want to be seen by others (your private self presented for public viewing)

3. How others see you (your public self)

4. The total you (for better or worse, your private and public selves combined)

Let's talk about this.

Ideally, all of these versions of you should be the same but, in reality, often they are not. When you are dealing with people, you cannot be certain if what you are seeing is what you are getting.

In the very beginning of the book, we talked about the word "I" and how we like to think of ourselves as a singular identity, but the truth is we have multiple aspects to ourselves, and they compete with one another.

Who are you really? Are you your private or your public self? Neither? Both?

Let's take a hypothetical example of a comedic actor. In private, let's say he is traumatically shy and prone to severe depression and drinking. This is his private self.

Now he is also a famous actor and is usually cast in comedy roles. His fans adore him and could never imagine him as depressed. It goes against everything they know about him. This is his public self.

Now this actor is also aware he is depressed and knows this is at odds with how his fans see him. He knows if the word got out that "Mr. Funny Man" was depressed it could hurt his career, so he is careful how he presents himself to others. He knows how he wants to be perceived and won't let anyone outside his family know of his problems. He wants to be seen as happy, so he fakes it. This is how he wants to be seen by others.

Now this actor has an agent, and the agent is aware of the discrepancy between the actor's private and public selves. He is constantly worried about the public discovering the actor's private self. Since the agent can see the interplay between the private and public selves, he has a front-row seat and can appreciate the actor's complete situation—this is the total self.

Now let's bring it down a level and talk about you.

We honestly believe happiness can only be realized when your public and private selves are in alignment. We don't believe you can find true happiness if you are one way in private and another way in public. Throughout this book, we have been advocating for you to get out and interact with others. We have been asking for you to bring other people into your life and to find something you feel passionate about and use that to do something for others.

But if who you are in private is somebody different from who you are pretending to be in public, then who are you doing this for? Who is the real you?

To be happy, you have to include your public and private selves in the deal; otherwise, your happiness will be nothing more than a ruse.

We realize it might take time and effort to bring your public and private selves into line, but it is something that needs to be done if you are to have long-lasting happiness.

CHAPTER 50
STAY HUMBLE

"Humility makes great mean twice honorable."
Benjamin Franklin

In one of the upcoming sections, we are going to be talking about key thoughts to keep you balanced and grounded. One of the keys is keeping in mind you are part of a bigger picture you cannot see.

This idea is nicely conveyed in the parable of the blind men and the elephant. In this story, six men are led to an elephant and asked to describe what they experience. Each man is led to a different part of the elephant—one to the tail, one to the trunk, another to the leg, another to the tusk, another to the ear, and another sits on top.

When they are asked to describe what the elephant is, each man describes something different.

All the men are right, yet all are wrong. Each man is correct in his perception but wrong about the overall picture.

In this parable, the elephant represents truth or reality, and the blind men represent us, humanity.

We can be correct in what we perceive, but we only perceive a part of the picture; therefore, we need to be cautious in the conclusions we draw. Not only that, but we have to be aware that different points of view are as valid as our own.

This is why humility is so important.

Someone who is humble is aware there are forces at work beyond his or her awareness. A humble person is aware there is a bigger picture he or she cannot see. For this reason, humble people do not make false accusations. They do not present opinion as fact. They do not speak out of turn or disrespect others. They do not brag or take credit for things they only played a part in.

In other words, humble people get it! They do what they have to, but they don't gloat or brag or rub things in people's faces. They are aware life is a mystery they will never unravel and don't pretend to have all the answers.

Keep in mind your place in the universe, and it will go a long way toward keeping you balanced in life.

CHAPTER 51
SEE GOOD THINGS IN BAD

"What seems to us as bitter trials are often blessings in disguise."
Oscar Wilde

The ability to see good things in a difficult situation is an excellent skill to have because no matter how hard you try to think positively, life can still send disappointments your way.

What can you do to prepare yourself for them?

First, we recommend getting busy with the suggestions we are making in this book. Get your goals set, start taking positive actions, reach out to others, make time for yourself, and follow your passion. These things will help plant you on solid ground.

Second, and this is the key point of this section, you need to understand good things often come out of disappointments and failures.

Let's look at an example.

Let's say you have been working for a company for several years and have been a faithful employee. You do your job, you do it well, and have always been a team player who looks out for the interests of the company. Every year you receive an annual evaluation and get a raise. The raises aren't much, but you have come to count on them and take them as a sign your employer appreciates your contributions. Then one year, the same as the others, you receive yet another favorable evaluation, but you are told there is no raise because times are tight. You let it go initially but after you learn the company's executives are continuing to reward themselves handsomely with bonuses, the situation begins to upset you.

Soon you find yourself becoming increasingly bitter and resentful until one day you reach the realization it is time for you to move on and start your own business. You start developing the business at night and on weekends and ultimately, your new venture becomes a huge success. This allows you to quit your job, do what you enjoy, and spend more time with your family, which leaves you happier and more fulfilled than ever.

If you had been given your usual raise, you probably would have continued on as always, year after year, making no changes, taking no risks, and being the same old you. But once something bad happened, as demoralizing as it was, it spurned you to make changes you should have made earlier. The result was a happier and more successful you!

Something unfortunate *needed to happen* before something good could. That's a curious phenomenon, but we have seen it happen so many times, it leads us to believe it is a universal and cosmic principle we don't fully understand.

It isn't much different from a forest fire that destroys thousands of acres of trees and brush, but in the end, clears the way for new growth and development.

In order to guard against the punches the world is bound to throw your way, you need to remember that not only do good things follow a setback, sometimes a setback *has to happen* for a lucky break to follow. The bad can precipitate the good.

If you come to believe in this principle enough, you might get yourself to a place where you don't mind setbacks because you know something good is probably right around the corner. Of course, we don't want you actually wishing for setbacks! We just want you to realize there is often a silver lining to some of the biggest disappointments life hands us.

CHAPTER 52
REMEMBER THESE KEY THOUGHTS

"A thought, even a possibility, can shatter and transform us."
Friedrich Nietzsche

In the preceding sections, we have been talking about thoughts and how they can influence your emotions. We, of course, have an obvious bias toward action but do not want to minimize the importance of deliberation. You need to take time, think about your passions, what is important to you and what your goals should be. But after that, after you have considered all that, you have to stop thinking and take action. Thinking is a good thing but too much is not.

But with all that said, we still believe in the power of thinking to control our emotions and protect us from the uncertainties life can send our way. And after several years of considering this problem, we have come up with three important thoughts.

These three thoughts will help keep you balanced and humble as you make your way through life and encounter challenges and problems. We believe these thoughts are the key to keeping a level head and staying balanced when dealing with others.

The three key thoughts are as follows:

1. Things are not always what they appear to be.

2. Perception is not the same as reality.

3. Knowledge is partial.

These three thoughts are derived from the parable of the blind men and the elephant. And that parable, in essence, captures the keys to the human condition—we only have partial knowledge but still have to make whole decisions.

In our opinion, most of the problems in today's world are not only man-made, but they are made worse by people who seem to think they have the whole picture when, in fact, they only have a part of it.

This happens on a smaller, individual level too.

We see one little thing and jump to all kinds of conclusions about it. We seldom take the time to slow down, question the accuracy of our information, and make decisions considering the fact we could be operating on bad or limited information.

If you think about it, acting on partial or inaccurate information is one of the biggest mistakes you could ever make, yet we do it all the time. How many times have you done something quickly based on what somebody told you and later found out the information was wrong? How did you feel? How would things have been different if you had stepped back for a moment and questioned the information or realized how limited it was? How different would your actions have been?

One of the effects will be to slow you down but in a good way! You will slow down because if you realize you only have partial information, then it will take you longer to factor the unknowns into your decision making. Knowing you don't know critical information is helpful because it makes you proceed carefully and cautiously. Just think—how dangerous is someone who thinks they know everything when you know they don't? Pretty dangerous, right? That's not the person you want to be!

Awareness of these guiding principles will keep you humble, safe, and balanced in a world that is becoming unpredictable.

CHAPTER 53
YOUR ENERGY IS ETERNAL

"What we can reach is far beyond our grasp."
The Authors

People are a mystery. We know so much and so little. We can do so many things or nothing at all. We have so much to offer each other, yet we talk ourselves out of it. We are a puzzle.

But if you get down to what we are made of, what will you find? Who are we really?

Of course, that's a question people have been asking for centuries and while we can't be certain we know the answer, we would like to give it our best shot.

We would like to start by acknowledging the obvious: We exist as physical beings in a physical world.

We see things, hear sounds, feel pain, and get hungry and thirsty and cold. Drilling right down to the basics, we are made of atoms—electrons, neutrons, and protons. When you examine us in a laboratory, we are electro-mechanical beings who give and take energy. That *is* who we are. That is how we are built. There's no denying the physics.

And as physical beings we interact with others and our environment by receiving and sending energy. We take and absorb energy from the environment and give energy in return. Transmitting energy is as necessary for our survival as is receiving it. In fact, since we are built of atoms and atoms are built of electrons, you might even say we exist as *electron*ic beings whose primary purpose is to transmit and receive energy.

What are we saying?

Think about speech. The human voice generates frequencies between 80 and 1,100 cycles per second. This is wave energy that travels through the atmosphere and is available for reception by anyone and anything capable of receiving it.

In short, our voices are perfectly designed to transmit energy and exist for that purpose alone.

Now what do we do with this ability? What is one of the first things we do as soon as we can?

We create technologies to amplify it even more! That's right. We invent microphones, megaphones, radio, and television and then broadcast our voices even farther and wider. And not just a little farther—a lot farther.

AM radio stations take our voices and generate frequencies over one million cycles per second. FM stations take our voices up to 108 million cycles per second and can even broadcast the signal into space.

What's happening here is more than just business and innovation.

This is us doing what we were made to do—sending and receiving energy.

If we exist as electronic beings whose primary purpose is to transmit and receive energy, then it makes sense we would naturally build on those innate functions and extend them as far as we could.

Our technology, in that sense, is an extension of who we are.

Now if you can accept this line of reasoning, then it isn't much of a step to believe everything we say, everything we do, and everything we think is a form of energy we are transmitting to the world.

But think about this.

In the previous sections, we made the point we can never know the whole picture and can only know parts and pieces. In fact, everything we know is partial. And if you believe that, then this would also suggest: *We don't know what happens to the energy we transmit.*

Once you say something, you are only aware of what you can see and hear. You have no way of knowing how what you said influenced the receivers, what they did with that information later, or even who all the receivers were. You cannot know the ultimate effect of what you said or what other effects it might have had. You can only know you said it. You have no way of tracking it.

After we say or do anything, after that energy is released, we have no control over it and no way to know where it goes. But as energy it goes on forever!

Everything you say and do and even think is released as energy into the world. That energy, once released, is beyond your control and can affect millions and millions of people forever. And you would not have any way of knowing where it all finally ended. You could not know. Released energy knows no boundaries and this is why we say your energy is eternal, or more precisely, the energy you transmit goes on forever.

So what does this mean in the grand scheme of things?

It means what you have to say matters. It means what you do matters. It means what you think matters.

What you do and say is important because it is releasing energy into the world and affecting countless people in ways you cannot imagine. It means you should take pride in yourself and what you say and what you do because it is significant and powerful and potentially eternal.

Think of all the times you have said something and later learned how someone completely misinterpreted it. Didn't it make you think twice about the power of your words?

Let's put it another way.

Imagine you are given ten minutes on national television to talk about why you love your family. You use your time to talk about all the special moments you've had with them and all the things they do that make you proud. And let's say it is the most eloquent speech of your life. And then, after you are done "transmitting" your energy to millions and millions of people, what effect do you think that might have had? How many lives do you think you might have touched? We have a feeling you know the answer.

On a much smaller scale though, when you are walking by someone, and you smile, you are transmitting positive energy, and if he or she smiles back, then they have returned energy to you, and you both go on your way. And now you feel better and that person feels better and if that energy is released or broadcast again, then it continues making a difference far beyond what you could have ever imagined.

Think about this for a moment.

From time to time, you have probably seen an inspirational quote attributed to someone who is unknown. (We have a couple of quotes like that in this very book!) Now what is that all about? Did the people not know they were being quoted? Did the original credit get lost in time? Either way, the fact is someone said something that created a positive chain reaction far beyond what that person could have ever known or imagined. And so their words live on without anyone knowing when or where the chain ends or if it even ends at all.

It's amazing really. A total amazing mystery. And you can be, if you so choose, right in the middle of it all, making it happen and creating a better world for everyone.

CHAPTER 54
END EACH DAY WITH A POSITIVE BROADCAST

"A man is but the product of his thoughts what he thinks, he becomes."
Mohandas Karamchand Gandhi

We have come a long way since we started and believe it is only appropriate to end on a positive note. We started with you as your own worst enemy and want to leave with you as your own best friend. That's the way it should be because that's the way you'll stay happy. You are the only one who knows what's happening on the inside, so you have to watch out for yourself and be your best friend.

The world is a tough place, but you are also tougher than you think. You've made it this far in life, so you must be doing some things right. There are many roads to happiness, and we are only giving you possibilities to try. We believe the key is taking action and setting goals you truly believe in and can accomplish. We believe doing good things for others is the most important key, and true happiness is a constant work in progress, never done or completed with always more to try.

So we want to leave you with one last suggestion and that is to end each day as if you were a television station signing off at the end of the evening with a positive word or note.

We want you to end each day, as it began, with a kind gesture, overture, or word.

It can be to yourself, someone in your family, a close friend, or even a higher power. You should make that final gesture every night because it is your final broadcast that completes the day.

If it is true we remember beginnings and endings, then what better time is there to do something positive than at the beginning and ending of each day?

If we can leave you with one final point, it is simply this:

While staying positive is a daily challenge, it opens the world up, makes it bigger and full of possibilities. Staying negative, while much easier to do, makes the world smaller and closes everything in around you.

And so, no matter how difficult it seems to keep moving in a positive direction every day, always remember that it *is* the right road to be on, and the one that will lead to true happiness. It is the path worth taking and will pay off in time—it really will.

There is no one way to happiness; there are many. We sincerely hope you find the one that works best for you. It takes time and effort, but it is most certainly time well spent.

APPENDICES

APPENDIX 1
POSITIVE BEHAVIORS YOU CAN DO NOW

Start a garden and share what you grow

Clean out your kitchen and find items to donate to a food bank

Paint over graffiti in your neighborhood or community

Donate or buy books for your local library

Return your shopping cart to the collection area

Pick up trash in your neighborhood or on the side of the road

Offer to help an elderly neighbor who needs help

Sell something and donate half of the money to your favorite charity

Be quiet and respectful of your neighbors

Campaign for a candidate you believe in

Volunteer at a shelter

Create a t-shirt with a positive message and wear it in public

Make a list of birth dates for everyone who is important to you and do something special for each person's birthday

Post a positive story on the internet

Find three inspirational quotes and share them with someone

Send a thank-you note to someone who has helped you

APPENDIX 2
ENJOYABLE THINGS TO DO

Watch a sunrise

Go to a zoo and check out the exhibits

Go to a park and have a picnic

Go see a matinee

Get a coffee drink and people watch

Take a hike somewhere new

Take a long drive in the country

Watch a sunset

Visit some art galleries

Try a new restaurant

Go listen to some live music

Go watch a moonrise and take a light snack

Try your hand at playing a guitar or ukulele

Listen to some calm and relaxing music

Take a walk on the beach

Go swimming or just lounge around by a pool

APPENDIX 3
NICE LITTLE THINGS YOU CAN DO FOR OTHERS

Smile

Hold a door open for someone

Get to work early and put out treats for your coworkers

Email an inspiring story to others

Make a home-cooked meal for someone you care about

Invite someone over for dinner

Give a copy of your favorite book to someone

Let someone with fewer groceries go in front of you

Put extra change in the change cup at stores

Let someone who is trying to cross a street go first

Offer your seat to an elderly person

If you are going to a store, ask if anyone needs something

Hold an elevator door open even if you are in a rush

Offer your newspaper or magazine to someone instead of throwing it away

Give a flower to someone at random

Put a mint or candy under your loved one's pillow

APPENDIX 4
IDEAS FOR A PERSONAL LEGACY

Build a web site for a cause you believe in

Start a small or micro business employing others

Create a piece of art with a positive theme

Write a book with an inspirational message

Buy a memorial stone or brick for a loved one

Make a significant contribution to your favorite charity

Create a trust or foundation for a cause you believe in

Create a scholarship program

Amend your will or life insurance policy to include a charity of your choosing

Establish an activity center for foster children

Pay for someone's college education

Buy or build a house for someone who needs it

Find a cure for something

Raise a child who has solid values

Lobby Congress on an issue that affects your community

Mentor an at-risk teenager

Build a community center for the young and old to get together

APPENDIX 5
DAILY REMINDERS

Start each day with a positive thought

Do something you enjoy and include someone else

Take time to relax each day

Go for a walk each day

Make one person smile each day

Experience one inspirational thing a day

Remember these concepts in things you see everyday

Positive dream programming every night

End each day on a positive note

pass the smiles.com